Fundraising for Churches

Jane Grieve is currently Development Director at St John's College Durham, the college she first attended as a student. She graduated with a General Arts degree, and later returned to study for the university's Theology Certificate, after which she joined the staff as a Personal Tutor. Her latest responsibilities have included raising over £1 million in five years for a range of projects close to the heart of the college.

Married to David, an Anglican priest whom she met as a fellow undergraduate at St John's, she has three children. Outside church and family she has a great enthusiasm for all things equestrian and competes regularly in novice long distance riding events. She has a particular interest in rural ministry and affairs, and recently joined the Council of Durham Rural Community Council. She is a member of the Institute of Charity Fundraising Managers.

Fundraising for Churches

Jane Grieve

First published in Great Britain in 1999

Society for Promoting Christian Knowledge
Holy Trinity Church
Marylebone Road
London NW1 4DU

British Library Cataloguing-in-Publication Data

A catalogue record for this book is available from the British Library

ISBN 0-281-05058-9

Design by Gwyn Lewis

Printed in Great Britain by The Redwood Press, Trowbridge, Wiltshire

Contents

CONTENTS

Foreword

Most of us have a dream. In church life many dreams relate to new projects, new buildings or the chance to set up a new way of working. Inevitably many of them involve money. Too often our dreams turn to despair as the noughts are added to the figures involved. 'If only I had thousands of pounds . . .' This well-researched, practical book will help all of us turn our dreams into reality. The excuse that we do not know how to go about raising the funds is no longer adequate.

Having been involved directly and indirectly in Jane Grieve's work at St John's College, Durham, I am delighted, and amazed, that she has found the time to write this practical guide to fundraising, born out of her own experience: the benefit of success as well as the honesty of occasional failure. It is therefore a genuine pleasure and an honour to be asked to contribute a foreword to her book.

I hope that *Fundraising for Churches* will not only find a place on the shelves of every clerical study, but that a well-thumbed copy will be read by every member of the PCC or Church Council. If we all followed the advice contained in these pages we would avoid several mistakes, and learn how to raise funds successfully so that many cherished visions become a reality.

Jane writes from the practical experience of running the Development Campaign at St John's College, Durham, and as well as drawing examples from the college she has wisely added ten case studies from parish life across the county – with objectives as diverse as raising hundreds of thousands of pounds for planting a new church, remodelling or rebuilding a church and renovating an organ; providing funding for youth and community projects; and increasing the regular church income by selling a specially and appropriately named real ale (encouraging debate about responsible patterns of drinking in the process).

The result is a step-by-step guide that both describes the way to set up and run a successful campaign and provides an invaluable check-list at the end of each chapter enumerating the key points at every stage of the process. Her comprehensive coverage of the importance of preparation and planning, and of the different sources of income – for individuals and events, through trusts and companies to statutory funding (both EEG and Government-based) and the Lottery – will repay careful study. Her explanations of the language of the professional fundraiser from 'the Pareto Effect' to 'Donor Fatigue' make the science accessible to all.

Fundraising creates important questions for the committed Christian. Jane's biblical and ethical introduction and her repeated stress on the central importance of *relationships* ensure that the theological issues are not avoided. She helpfully analyses the ethical questions that accompany the raising of money in the modern world, and having weighed the issues invites the reader to form their own judgement through a series of practical but sharp questions.

To quote her own words:

> Both [fundraising and the gospel] are concerned with winning people to a new point of view, adjusting their priorities and seeking allegiance not just from their wallets, but to a very real degree from their hearts and minds.

I know Jane will feel her efforts will have been well rewarded if these pages help others to follow the path she herself has trodden in fulfilling that twin aim.

> You will glorify God by your obedience in acknowledging the gospel of Christ and by the generosity of your contribution . . . Thanks be to God for his inexpressible gift (2 Corinthians 9.13,15).

† *Ian Petriburg*
(Ian Cundy, Bishop of Peterborough)

Preface

Somewhat to my surprise I found myself employed in a full-time job for the first time in my life (as Development Director for St John's College Durham) at the grand old age of forty-something. The whole thing has taken me by surprise, taken my breath away. It takes my breath away every day I come into work, and another cheque has appeared in my pigeonhole or another project reaches completion.

My background lies out in the parishes of the Church of England. Ever since graduating from St John's in the mid-1970s I have been fully involved in a voluntary capacity in whichever parish my husband, an Anglican priest, happened to be serving at the time. Three very different parishes, in three different dioceses, have given a fairly wide perspective on the needs faced by many churches today.

My basic reason for producing this book is therefore to share what I have learned with those who are struggling to grow and develop in a Church context, but who are held back by that most mundane of reasons, lack of finance. I long for some of the lessons I have learned over the past few years to be of service to local churches and fellowships.

It remains to thank the many people who have helped me in the course of my work and who have influenced this book directly or indirectly through their advice or example (the flaws of course remain my responsibility alone). My husband and family bear the habitual ups and downs of a fundraiser's life with unbounded patience, equanimity and vital moral support. I have learned an enormous amount from my fellow fundraising professionals, especially those in the North East Group of the Institute of Charity Fundraising Managers. However, the most formative years of my life have been spent in different capacities within the unique institution that is St John's. Without it my life would have been the poorer in so many ways, and I would have had no story to share in this book. I hope that the chapters which follow will serve in some small way to express my thanks for all that I have received within its doors.

Jane Grieve
St John's College Durham

Introduction

This book falls naturally into four sections. I hope that you will find each one thought-provoking and of practical use as you seek to raise funds in your own special and unique situation. No one will experience exactly the same challenges or seek to meet exactly the same needs that face you, and no one will work in the same context with the same resources. However, many others have already trodden similar paths sharing aims very like your own, and you need not begin your task totally unprepared. Working through these sections successively will help you to be better equipped to fundraise effectively in your small corner of the church and the world. They are preceded by a summarized outline of practical steps.

Part One reveals just how much work there is to do before you even contemplate approaching your first potential donor or making public your fundraising plans. It is crucial not to underestimate the value of thorough and exhaustive planning, and of consultation at every level. Time-consuming and daunting it may sound, but the rewards will be reaped in due time. It makes sense to maximize your income, even if this means waiting a little longer for the pennies to roll in. Examples drawn from my experience are used to illustrate each chapter, followed by simple bullet points to use as a checklist.

Part Two provides the meat you may have been looking for when you bought this book – a description of the major sources of income you may be able to tap into in your fundraising, with practical hints about how to access them. They are very different, and you will need to pick and choose the ones which are right for you. Fundraising is not easy, but the information in this section should help you decide the most likely sources at your disposal, and to target them effectively. Once again, college examples are there to illuminate the theory, and a checklist of points to remember follows.

Part Three concentrates on the underlying ethical principles which exist, often unspoken and sometimes unsuspected, behind much fundraising activity. I have tried to highlight some of these principles in a non-prescriptive way, drawing attention to their existence but without identifying any one way forward which I personally might feel churches should follow. My aim is to stimulate prayerful thought about what is appropriate for your church and your community. You will have the task of applying these principles to your own context. I hope the issues I identify, the biblical themes I highlight and the discussion points I suggest will support you as you do this.

The fourth and final Part was a particular pleasure to write, as it highlighted just how much is going on already in the Church to bring visions and dreams to reality. I have chosen ten case studies drawn from real-life examples, although I have disguised the names and parishes who have so generously helped. These have been selected for their variety both of church and of fundraising task tackled.

You may know of further examples. If you do, talk to those involved! I have found both clergy and lay people keen to share what they have learned and without exception delighted to feel that their labours may be of benefit to the wider Church. It is my hope that one day you too will have a thrilling story to tell, and that the chapters which follow will have played their part in helping you turn many visions into reality.

Outline of practical steps

Groundwork (Chapters 1, 2)

Collective prayer and discernment
* Identify the task.
* Formulate a mission statement.

Defining the project
* Get clear about the direction of the project.
* Prioritize objectives.
* Identify the needs that the project will meet, and back this up with research.
* Commission a feasibility study.
* Produce costings (capital and revenue).

Planning
* Devise a strategy for realizing the project.
* Draft a business plan.

Building a base
* Consult widely.
* Look for partners, with similar aims.
* Look for supporters, to promote your cause.

Initiating the campaign (Chapters 3–10, 11–14)

Forming the team
* Choose one person as key fundraiser.
* Find a chairperson or figurehead.
* Name some patrons?
* Assemble a team of advisers.

* Form an executive committee.
* Enlist volunteers.

Identifying sources of help
* Look for contacts and supporters close at hand.
* Check out directories and the Internet.
* Invest in training.
* Consult agencies.
* Hire a consultant?

Preparing to go public
* Assemble the best arguments, statistics and letters of support to present the case for your project.
* Produce a variety of background documents to back up your main application.
* Make sure all your team know the case for funding inside-out.

Identifying potential funders
* Choose trusts whose criteria match your needs closely.
* Look for companies which might have an interest in helping.
* Consider European and national statutory sources.

Approaching potential funders
* Use all your contacts for insight and to provide an introduction.
* If they say no, try to leave a door open to re-apply in future.

Writing applications
* Treat recipients as individuals.
* Be positive.
* Be clear, logical and accurate.
* Decide what appendices to include.
* Check the application letter with someone who knows nothing about your work.
* Give thought to timing applications.

Targeting applications
* Work out how much you need.
* Plan how to spread your applications across the different categories of donor.

* Channel your energies to major gifts first.
* Make sure you ask for enough.

Running the campaign (Chapters 8–10, 15–18)

Ways of giving
* Consider the varied forms of direct giving.
* Take care in seeking major gifts.

Receiving different types of gift
* Follow best practices in handling cash.
* Promote tax-efficient ways of giving.
* Make use of gifts in kind.
* Include legacies, loans and pledges among possible ways of helping.

Administration
* Value good office and computing practices.
* Produce regular campaign progress reports.
* Process and acknowledge donations promptly.
* Follow the law and best practice in financial procedures.
* Be aware of the risk of fraud.

Considering additional options
* Events (Chapter 15).
* Media relations (Chapter 16).
* Merchandising (Chapter 17).

Ongoing considerations (Chapter 18).

PART ONE **PLANNING**

1 The institution

The Church and money

It seems to be a depressingly common perception today that the Church is in decline, and that its financial situation is a particular sign of a terminal malaise. Newspapers run articles on the decrease in active church membership, paralleled by the crisis affecting church finances. Most mainstream denominations seem equally affected.

If the Church is having trouble even paying its way today, how much more difficult is the task to raise £X thousands for important new projects? a church extension? a new member of staff? an exciting project to really get to grips with the social problems in the parish? – all in the name of Christ? It can seem such a battle, against odds of inertia and apathy, to pay the diocesan quota, let alone to dream of exciting new initiatives to take the Church out into the heart of the community and become relevant once more to the needs of real people.

Christians appear to come to terms with this unpalatable truth in a number of ways. A frequent reaction is to close ranks, cut cloth according to means, and prune ministry according to existing income. Sincere regret is expressed at such retrenchment, but no other options appear to be available. This can even be seen at a national level – reductions in numbers of clergy across the board and long interregnums to reduce the size of the payroll; and at individual church level no new outreach or developments, cutting the proportion given away or tithed, just concentrating on paying as much of the diocesan quota as can be afforded.

A second common reaction is to spiritualize the issue – if God really wants us to grow and make a greater impact, then all we need to do is ask and the blessings will follow. Lack of money must equal lack of faith or obvious disobedience. Sort these out and our problems will evaporate. Or perhaps it is just not God's will that x, y or z happen. Maybe we should have a series of prayer meetings or a sermon course on stewardship, and treat the outcome as guidance. Any other strategy is worldly.

I believe that both a feet-on-the ground realism and a head-in-the-clouds idealism have their place in authentic Christian living, but that one without the other can quickly lead to a discipleship that is out of balance. I would like to suggest a third way forward, which takes elements of both approaches, and blends them into a potent mixture of common sense and faith. We need enough basic realism to assess the situation as it is, but sufficient vision to see what might be.

Into battle!

There is no doubt that churches today face a great battle for survival. However, the Bible resounds with imagery of warfare – against injustice, social evils, all the works of the devil. The amazing perspective we are left with is that with God on our side, the weak, the feeble, the vastly outnumbered, can actually hope for victory. In the realm of finance as in every other area of church life that is an encouraging thought.

When the idea of a new fundraising drive for St John's College Durham was first suggested, we were advised early on to think in terms of a Development Campaign rather than a Fundraising Appeal. 'Appeals are for dead ducks and lost causes', we were told. A campaign, on the other hand, is undertaken for a worthwhile cause after due thought and consideration. That made sense to us, and ever after, those referring to the St John's College Appeal (as long as tact and sensitivity allowed!) would be gently corrected.

I like the term 'campaign', because it reminds me that I too am fighting in a battle – a battle to enable 13 worthwhile projects to happen, and to persuade people to part with their money in order to help. It reminds me that strategy, planning and realism are important. That knocks and reverses are inevitable, but that so are small day-to-day advances and triumphs. That perseverance and steadfastness will be needed, but that ultimately I am on the winning side. And when I get discouraged, there are plenty of biblical references to refer to for renewed inspiration!

Laying the foundations

I would argue that the time spent planning any fundraising campaign, however great or small, is the most important phase of all. Days, weeks, months before anyone is ever asked for any money, the foundations for

3

future success should be laid. They are crucial. Any suggestion that the planning phase can be short-circuited or avoided, any undue pressure for an immediate result, is putting the success of the whole venture in jeopardy. It is that important.

The planning process, if embarked upon thoroughly, can also have unexpected benefits for the life of any church. Many companies and corporate institutions have been encouraged in recent years to produce their 'mission statement' and use this as a springboard to develop a development plan for the next five to ten years ahead. Every church could usefully spend time going through a similar process, summarizing just what they are about, in maybe 20 words or less. It is interesting that the business world has actually hijacked Christian terminology to describe this process – it is a *mission* statement. Woe betide the church that ignores its own mission! Church members should be encouraged to come to a common mind about the basic mission they are called to carry out in their particular situation. Talking this through at an early stage ensures that everyone is starting from the same presuppositions and that effective communication is happening at the heart of the church community.

Years before my involvement as Development Director for St John's College, I remember the build-up to Mission England in 1984. At the time my husband was vicar of a small ex-mining community in County Durham, and the famous evangelist Billy Graham was soon due to visit Roker Park in Sunderland as part of his UK tour. I well remember part of the preparation process leading up to the visit, which involved church members taking a cool hard look at themselves, and asking 'Is my church worth joining?' Many folk with a lifetime of membership and service had never faced this issue in quite this way before. It was an illuminating process.

This is just the kind of exercise that should be undertaken before any major fundraising campaign. We need to know where we are before we can decide where we are going. The process should involve looking at every area of church life. A helpful approach could be to do this using what is known in management circles as a 'SWOT' analysis, looking in depth at Strengths, Weaknesses, Opportunities and Threats of each area of church life, making lists under each heading in order to arrive at a realistic picture of the current state of the whole institution.

Another useful approach could be to carry out a kind of 'internal audit'. Try to analyse who the church membership consists of, what natural gifts and talents are waiting to be tapped, what the needs of the local community are, what outreach is going on, what attempts are being made to serve the community. Which areas of church life are functioning well at present? Which seem to need a little bit of extra help? Some surprising facts may be revealed which will help the Church be more effective in its day-to-day ministry in the locality.

Getting the support of the whole institution

One key element to get right before even making a start on active fundraising is to have the understanding and support of the Church behind any scheme or plan. Church members will be the key ambassadors for any project that is taken on. They must be convinced of the need for a fundraising campaign and of the value of the cause or project for which funds are being raised. Objectively and subjectively, in hearts and in minds, the campaign must appear to them to be the right way forward.

This sense of common purpose is most likely to be arrived at through prayer over the issue that has inspired the campaign in the first place. It may begin with one man or woman's vision, tested by the wider Church and then adopted as God's way forward for a particular church community at a particular time. Without this sense of the 'rightness' of the task, and without wholehearted support of the Church as a whole, the inevitable times of testing and pressure will become too much. Courageous decisions will not be taken when necessary, the Church as a whole will give out an equivocal message to potential supporters from outside, and supporters will lose heart.

If a little time has been spent coming to a common mind about key aims and purposes, and researching the nature of the church fellowship and the impact it is currently having in the local community, two of the basic procedures necessary in drawing up a plan of action for the future have already been completed. The next stage is to scrutinize and test the dreams and visions. Or in more prosaic language, to make choices about the future direction the institution should take. Priorities should be set, and some aims identified to be achieved within the next three, five or ten years. These can be supported by specific objectives. It is good to involve as many people and as many areas of corporate life as possible, though tact and sensitivity may be needed when assessing the practicality of some of the wilder ideas thrown up by this process! Are these dreams achievable? Where might the resources come from, in manpower, in commitment, in money?

Formulating a strategy

The ultimate intention at this initial stage is to take the aims and objectives and to formulate a strategy to achieve them. This may involve setting targets, and listing the different kinds of resources that will be needed to have a realistic chance of achieving them. These resources will not only be financial. Any step forward which needs fundraising to take place to allow it to happen will need leadership, time, space, volunteers, enthusiasm and know-how to stand a chance of success – and an investment of some money to prime the pump and start the whole process off. For example a first survey of the different kinds of funding that might be available may be needed, and a strategy planned to show how it is intended to go about tapping into them. Strategy can be flexible, and can evolve and develop as the campaign proceeds, but to start off without one at all is one of the quickest ways that I know to burn oneself out to little or no effect.

It is often helpful to draw up a commonly agreed document that describes the life of the church in all its aspects, and which identifies and prioritizes different possible developments. It estimates the costs involved in terms of people, skills, material resources, time and money, and gives some indication as to where these might come from. Few funders will be willing to part with sums of money to any organization which does not present a coherent plan for the future, and cannot demonstrate a basic capability of seeing the plan through. A special working party drawn from the PCC, for example, and leadership from various church groupings, could present such a report to the church's AGM as part of the process.

College example: How it all started

St John's is not a wealthy college, as all those who have been connected to it over the years will attest. It was established in 1909 to provide an alternative location for prospective Anglican clergymen to receive a university education in the north of England. No wealthy patrons endowed it with sums of money or art treasures to secure its future. Its income has always come primarily from the fees paid by students and ordinands. No central block grants from the government or the Church. When it has sensed the need to grow or develop in a new direction it has had to find the funding to carry this out itself.

Over the decades since its formation the college grew and diversified, and now comprises St John's Hall, with some 350 undergraduates and postgraduates studying the full range of degrees available in the university, and Cranmer Hall, with around 100 men and women training for lay and ordained full-time church work in the Anglican and Methodist Churches. A far cry from the tiny handful of serious gowned and mortar-boarded staff and students who appear in the first college photograph of 1910.

In the 1980s, in response to a period of growth, the college had undertaken a highly successful development campaign under the then principal Dr Ruth Etchells, refurbishing many areas of the college, and building a new hall large enough to accommodate the whole college community at one time. As another wave of expansion swept across higher education in the early 1990s, it seemed right to look again at the essence of what St John's was about as a community and what made it such a distinctive place to study, and to examine the feasibility of a new campaign.

In January 1992 a new principal was appointed to the college. David Day is an inspirational leader, a dynamic enthusiast and an able communicator. In the early months after his appointment he encouraged members of the college community to look at every area of college life and to dream dreams about the possibilities for growth and development over the next few years. Out of this process a long vision document evolved, and 13 different projects crystallized to become the focus of the new college development campaign.

At first each project appeared isolated, separate and distinct. I am grateful for a perceptive member of the college's governing body who listened to all the dreams and bright ideas, and in a few simple sentences drew them together into a clear and coherent structure which was eventually used as the basis for all our publicity and presentations. Thirteen projects in fact naturally gravitated into four strands, each reflecting important areas of the life of the college and building on existing strengths. The strands highlighted in turn mission, the community, international relations and student welfare. In the cold light of day it seemed daunting – fundraising for one project at a time can be hard enough; fundraising for 13 seemed an enormous task.

I have had cause to be thankful many many times for the careful thought and prayer which went into the early planning, especially for a particular meeting where the staff joined together to pray about the campaign and to decide whether this was indeed the right way forward. For me this resulted in a deep conviction that we as a college and I as

7

the fundraiser were receiving a specific call to action. These early steps along the way were important. We emerged as a college community convinced of the value of our projects, and committed to seeing them become reality.

Points to remember

* Pray.

* Analyse the current state of church life and areas of ministry.

* Get the approval of the whole church.

* Formulate a 'mission statement'.

* Draw up a development plan: identify aims and objectives, dreams and visions.

* Set your priorities.

* Devise a strategy: how your aims will be achieved.

---

2 The project

When you have decided in broad terms upon your mission as outlined in the previous chapter, the task has only just begun. Fundraising is no easy enterprise, as anyone who sees a directory of charitable trusts in the library, fires out a few speculative applications and sits back waiting for the money to roll in will soon discover. A lot of heartache can be saved by spending some time objectively assessing the strengths and weaknesses of your project before you even think of asking anyone for their support.

Is there a real need?
Many of the potential sources of funding whom you will approach in the course of a fundraising campaign are adept at summing-up a project application in minutes, if not seconds, using a variety of criteria. Near the top of their list will be the question 'Is there a real need for this project?' If you don't really believe that there is such a need, it would be better for everyone concerned to abandon the idea, however close it is to your heart, right at the start. Astute donors will not give to you anyway, and even if your fundraising does achieve some success, you may well be taking funds that would be better used elsewhere for some more worthy cause. Even if by some chance you get the funding you need, and your project becomes reality, it will soon be obvious to all that it was not really necessary and your credibility for future fundraising efforts will be damaged.

If you do believe it is needed, the hard work of actually proving it becomes one of your first priorities. Do your research and marshal your statistics. Find out first if anyone else has already carried out surveys that will save you the legwork of doing your own research, for instance into the needs of the community you are hoping to serve. Your local council may be of help here. For example, what is the unemployment rate in your area? Within that, what is the level of youth unemployment? Crime statistics? Other commonly recognized indicators of de-

9

privation? Is anyone else already trying to achieve the same end as your project? Will your project meet a need that no one else is reaching at this moment in time?

If no one else has carried out a survey that delivers all the information you feel you need, then consider carrying out one of your own. Church members may be able to help in this; it's possible for instance that students at school or college could do some of the work as part of an educational project. Aspects surveyed can include general demographic information on the types of housing, social bands of the local population, employment patterns, income levels of the area, broken down as far as possible into sub-areas of your parish or community. It could go on to look at the needs of your community and what provision already exists, from statutory and other voluntary bodies. When arguing your case to potential funders, it is good to be able to underline the need for your project with hard facts, and to emphasize that you will not be duplicating any other initiatives.

Seek out partners

It may even be that your research turns up another church or organization already undertaking the kind of work you have in mind, and that a shared approach in partnership would be more appropriate. A joint approach may provide a more effective solution to the problem, and can also strengthen your hand in making applications. Ask local people if they welcome your plans. Check for feedback that your own church members or the regular supporters of your organization continue to feel that the project is right. Other wider church sources may also be of help; those in the diocese, circuit or region who have expertise in urban affairs, rural affairs, church buildings, or any specialist ministry you are hoping to explore may have words of wisdom to share. Consider whether any respected sources of this kind of information might be willing to write a letter of support for your application, which could be appended to it when you send it off. Possibilities might include your MP, MEP, local councillors, community leaders and church leaders. Writing to them to ask for their help will at the very least raise awareness of your plans among some very influential people.

Spend a little time thinking about the beneficiaries of your project. What solutions are you offering to their needs? What difference will your project make to the quality of their lives? Do they actually want your help? How will society as a whole benefit? Are there any personal stories that it would be appropriate to use (with permission, and perhaps anonymously) to bring your evidence to life? Learn all your arguments so they become part of your life, and it becomes instinctive to summon them to strengthen your case whenever necessary. It's a little like St Paul's injunction that we always be ready to give a reason for the hope that is within us.

Feasibility study

Undertaking a serious feasibility study can be helpful at this stage, both for your own planning and to provide extra reassurance to funders that their money will not be wasted if they give it to you. Such a study might cover the situation as it is now, describe ways in which the project will meet identified needs and how possible problems that may arise will be dealt with, and outline achievable targets for the first year or two of operations. A clear and well-thought-out document should result, which should be of use not only in the fundraising stage but also in the early months and years of the project's life. If you don't feel able to undertake such a study on your own, external help is well worth while, perhaps commissioned from a professional fundraiser, or from others experienced in the field your project covers, perhaps from similar work elsewhere in the country. If you have a local further education college or university nearby, there may be students who could carry this out as part of their coursework for a dissertation or thesis.

Learn from others!

At the very least, talk to as many people as possible who have undertaken similar projects, especially where the context is similar to your own; telephone conversations could be followed by visits in some cases. Learn from the mistakes others may have made. Try to predict the problems and work through the answers before you are asked embarrassing questions by funders. Involve as many of your supporters as possible in this process as it will enormously help their understanding of what you are trying to achieve, and will make them more effective as advocates for your cause.

Finances

Your study should also include a brief business plan, showing that the finances will be on a sound footing. This should list all conceivable projected income and expenditure, and show how the books will balance. It goes without saying that all costs should be as accurate as possible. If

11

a surplus is budgeted for, which can be invested back into the project to help it grow, or be transferred back to the church or parent organization to support the mainstream work of the institution, this may reassure potential funders that the project has a sound financial basis. They may be reassured to know that even if all your rosy predictions for income do not quite materialize, you should at least be able to break even. Your church treasurer, or any members of the church who are used to budgets and business plans in their work, may be able to help you draw up your business plan coherently and in a suitable format.

Remember there are two main funding issues: how to fund the project in its initial stages and kick-start it into existence (usually one-off capital costs), and the annual expenses of keeping the project going once you have started it all up (revenue costs). Funders are understandably wary of giving money to exciting projects, which then fade to nothing within months.

Evaluation and monitoring

As well as the finances, there can also be logistical problems in administering a new project. Its progress should be closely monitored and evaluated. Who will oversee the initial phase as things get up and running? And who will take over the administration long term? Will success bring its own problems in terms of increased demands on paid staff or volunteers? If so, where will the increased resources needed come from?

A mechanism should be built into the project so that its progress can be evaluated, and progress measured against the original predictions. Failure to meet these does not necessarily indicate failure of the project; it may have more to do with the quality of your original estimates! However, you should know why the originally expected results did not materialize, and be able to explain this lucidly and honestly to funders.

College example: The Centre for Christian Communication

The first strand of the college development campaign involved the provision of resources for mission, not only for ourselves but for the wider Church, reflected in three interlocking projects: the Cross Gate Centre (the reopening of a boarded-up former hospital wardblock in the city centre), which would among other things provide a home for the Centre for Christian Communication, and within which a specific area would be devoted to the creation of a Multi-Media Studio. In other words we were seeking funding for the building, staff salaries and specialized equipment.

Our plans coincided with further media reports of church decline and complaints about the ability of church leaders and clergy to communicate effectively. It seemed that a raw nerve had been exposed in this area, universally acknowledged but being ineffectively treated. Everyone we spoke to also agreed that there was a particular need for such a facility accessible to lay and ordained church leaders across the north of England. Certainly no one else in the region was addressing this precise need in this way. Our position as the main Anglican theological college for the north of England meant that we were well placed geographically to take on such a project, with well-established networks of contacts and acknowledged expertise in theological education.

Informal discussions with those involved in Christian communication elsewhere in the country confirmed our belief that we would be meeting a real need for churches of all denominations if this centre became reality. We began to work on a business plan to test the viability of the project. It was relatively easy to cost the salaries involved; harder to identify the equipment that the centre would need. At first the dream was of high specification television and radio studios, with state of the art technology – until a highly placed television executive told us that that was the last thing we should be thinking of! Discretion and wise advice helped us to see that far more valuable would be flexible space with lower specification equipment more easily available to ordinary groups – a youth group perhaps wanting to make a video to show at a special service, or a church wanting to use a range of media to produce their own baptism preparation course.

When formulating the business plan for the Centre for Christian Communication, we had one important factor in our favour. The centre itself would begin to generate some income as its operations got underway. However, if the centre's facilities were to be priced at an affordable rate for churches and other groups from the voluntary sector, this income would never be enough to completely underwrite the salaries needed to run it. Nor was it likely that enough income would be generated to cover depreciation of equipment or to continually reinvest in further equipment as technological advances continued. The college itself could not divert income to keep the centre afloat, being obliged to use all its fee income received from students to run its core operations. However, income could legitimately be diverted from surpluses generated by other activities elsewhere in the Cross Gate Centre building. This allowed us to argue that the centre would not ultimately have to break even in order to be viable, giving a much greater margin for experimentation as it built its reputation in the early months and years.

While the campaign was still in its confidential stage, discussions took place with a major charitable trust that had generously funded the college in the past. Despite the feeling among some trustees that the college had received its fair share from them on earlier occasions, the fact that the plans for the Centre for Christian Communication were seen as being a resource for the whole region and not just for the college led to the decision to give a lump sum towards the refurbishment of the building and to pledge half the director's salary for five years, leaving the college to find another donor to supply the other half. Happily, a representative of another major Christian trust attended the public launch of the campaign in London, and suggested that the principal submit a formal application for funding for the other half. Part-funding for three years was approved by the trustees some months later, and in September that year the first director, Mr Geoffrey Stevenson, was appointed. The project had moved fully from vision to reality.

One of the provisos made by the second trust was that the project be monitored in depth in order to reveal lessons and pointers that might be useful for other charities and projects elsewhere in the country. The college was delighted to agree to this, and has been pleased to continue to work with the trust to put this into practice. It is good to know that lessons learned through the work of the centre will have an even wider application and benefit through this process.

Points to remember

* Take time to prepare and consult.

* Gather supporting statistics as widely as possible.

* Look for partners.

* Consider a feasibility study.

* Consult those with similar experience.

* Draft a business plan laying out the finances.

* Build in effective monitoring of progress, and evaluation of achievements.

---

3 The home team

Effective fundraising is rarely the result of one person's efforts. Behind every successful fundraiser lies a host of other individuals who have provided vital links in the chain leading to each donation. The 'Home Team' – those who identify with your cause and are willing to exert themselves on your behalf – are vital. They can make or break the fundraising effort.

Any fundraising operation of more than the smallest proportions will benefit from a well-defined and thought-out committee structure. Additional meetings are a necessary evil of any fundraising campaign – but in the right hands they can be motivating forces for ever greater efforts rather than yawn-inducing consumers of entire evenings at a stroke.

The fundraiser

It is advisable that one person takes ultimate responsibility for actually carrying out the fundraising. This may be the minister or vicar of the parish, in which case he or she will need ample secretarial and administrative back-up to help carry out this crucial role alongside the everyday demands of ministry. It may be a volunteer within the congregation, who has some experience of fundraising or work of some kind within the charitable sector. It may be a newly retired business person, with energy and ability to throw into a project for which they feel a genuine personal commitment. It certainly does not have to be a fundraising professional, although if you can find a professional fundraiser who understands your ethos and shares a belief in your project, it is no bad thing to engage professional advice if your means can possibly allow it. However, the personality and commitment of the person involved are vital; they must be able to convey genuine enthusiasm to potential funders, and inspire confidence in the organization for which they are working.

Channels of communication must always be open between the fundraiser and the body for whom he or she is working. All approaches for funding must be funnelled through him or her. The fundraiser should sit at the centre of the whole network of contacts and be absolutely sure who has been spoken to about what at each stage of the campaign. A hasty or ill-conceived conversation with a potential donor by someone on the fringes of the organization might be enough to convey a false impression of your work and what you are trying to do, or might elicit a small token donation when you had really hoped for a substantial sum. Your credibility as an efficient, reliable set-up can be compromised if the left hand doesn't appear to know what the right hand is doing.

Campaign chair

Another key role may be played by a campaign chairperson. To have a fundraiser and chairperson working in tandem can lift some of the pressure and work burden from the fundraiser's shoulders, and if you choose a locally known and respected individual, you can add a great deal of prestige and credibility to your cause, finding that some doors can be opened for you which would have remained firmly shut if the fundraiser alone had tried to give them a push.

The qualities required of this paragon are many, and the search for the right person may take a long time, but the right choice will ultimately reap dividends. He or she will be a person of vision. They will have a genuine interest, even a burning commitment to your cause. They will bring a number of contacts on board in their wake. They will be good communicators, comfortable commending your cause to the public and in the press. They will be able to motivate the rest of the team whether things are going badly or well. They will be effective chairers of meetings, able to handle a busy agenda, allow debate, sum-up effectively and make decisions.

Go for the person who brings as many of these qualities as possible to the role, and whom the fundraiser feels able to work with in the practical nitty gritty and minutiae of everyday life in the campaign. It is important that there is complete confidence in the person in question, and that those involved in the campaign feel comfortable and able to share with them at a deep level through both heady success and deep discouragements.

A newly retired Christian business executive might fit the bill in some instances; used to chairing meetings and getting things done, with a number of contacts still in the corporate world, but with spiritual depth and sensitivity to the fact that there are important distinctions between the ways that businesses and churches operate. The chairperson's role is a hands-on one, and will demand much in time and effort. Whatever their past role in life, they should have gifts of leadership, communication and time, and exude integrity and enthusiasm for your cause.

Patrons
Backing up the chairperson there may be one or more patrons. These will be names to catch the eye, which immediately command respect. They may do little in practical terms, but should be willing at least to make their support public, to put their names to letters of support and on any literature you produce, and to take an informed interest in your progress.

Campaign committee
Alongside the fundraiser and chairperson you will need other members of a campaign committee, chosen for their experience, commitment and ability. If, for example, the vicar is not either chief designated fundraiser or chairperson, it is obviously vital that he or she is on the committee, and is aware that the campaign will demand a substantial time commitment from them. Many people will expect to deal with the vicar directly in all things connected to the campaign, even if capable laypeople actually have the greater responsibilities for fundraising or running the necessary committees. It is likely that at least one churchwarden, steward or elder will be involved, and that an automatic member should be the church treasurer. Other church members with relevant gifts and experience should be drafted in, e.g. those whose professional life, qualifications or experience will be valuable. Everyone on the committee should be there with a job to do, and with the expectation that they will pull their weight. Some people may be co-opted with a specific role in mind, and be members for a limited length of time, rather than being asked to take on an open-ended time commitment that might last for months or even years.

The obvious biblical pattern for the working of such a committee lies in the image of the body – many parts, many members, all different, all with a vital role to play for the good of the whole. Harmonious relationships are so important, as in every area of church life. Keeping close to the original vision is important and will ease the tensions in many a fraught committee meeting. Shared acts of worship will help keep the vision bright and relationships sweet.

Advisory group

A substantial campaign will obviously demand a high level of commitment during its lifetime. It may be worth considering dividing the committee into two groups, with slightly different roles and responsibilities. An executive or steering group would have the responsibility to drive the campaign along, to take policy decisions on issues as they arise, and to run the day-to-day affairs of the campaign. It would meet regularly to monitor progress. It could be supported by a larger group, with a brief to support and advise. Individuals would be invited to join it because of some specific recognized contribution they could make, possibly for a specific phase of the campaign. It could be an area of expertise, or a particular network of contacts to whom they could introduce the campaign. They could be guaranteed a limited time commitment, e.g. full meetings no more than two or three times a year, but agree to be available to discuss progress informally and to offer advice individually to members of the main committee more frequently as need arises on a one-to-one basis.

Volunteers

Within the church, if the whole church body has approved the project, there may be a number of active volunteers who can be called upon to help in practical ways. These might include volunteering to help with the administration of the campaign, stuffing envelopes, distributing literature, helping at fundraising events. Working together with a common purpose for something that they feel is worthwhile can be a very positive experience for some, and can also be a means to draw them closer into the mainstream life of the Church.

However, be aware that working with volunteers can bring problems. Some may have a perspective on their own gifts and abilities that may be at variance with your own! Some may have high expectations of the sort of work that is needed and be distinctly crestfallen at being asked to do yet more photocopying, routine filing and boring envelope-stuffing. Some may be unreliable and only appear intermittently because it is not a 'proper' job. Some may not know enough about the ins and outs of the campaign to be able to answer random telephone queries from potential funders. Others may bring petty rivalries or jealousies with them into the campaign office. Using volunteers usually implies a need for conscious management of their work by the fundraiser or other campaign staff in order to channel their contribution positively. However, highly motivated, committed and able volunteers are the salt of the earth and most fundraising ventures could not do without them.

Natural supporters

This can also be true for many people out in the community who may support the work of the Church wholeheartedly, but who for whatever reason are not practising churchgoers. A campaign like this can actually provide an ideal opportunity for sympathizers and supporters to be drawn closer into the life of the Church, and to form solid relationships with existing church members, which may make it easier for them to cross the threshold to participate in worship at some point in the future. Particularly in a church context, a fundraising campaign should never be the be-all and end-all of life, and indeed can actually create additional opportunities to share what the Church is all about to those around.

College example: Creating the structures

The St John's College campaign broadly followed the structure outlined above. I was already working for the college as personal tutor to undergraduates, with additional responsibility for maintaining address lists and keeping in touch with former students. It seemed to the senior staff to be a natural progression to build on this background and the esoteric knowledge arising out of twenty years of association with the college by asking me to take on some fundraising responsibilities. It was agreed that a recent graduate of the college should be recruited to provide administrative backup.

The principal in turn accepted that a substantial part of his own time should be devoted to campaign issues, especially when potential donors expected to deal with the person at the top! This is a common expectation in corporate affairs, and only to be expected when large donations are on the agenda. David Day's own consummate communication skills enable him to play his part to perfection. The hunt for a high-profile chairman ended when Roger Kingdon, a retired local businessman and former chairman of Teesside Development Corporation, decided to throw in his lot with us, to our great benefit and advantage. Roger excels in motivating the team, chairing meetings with the minimum of wasted time and providing a positive public profile for St John's. The Archbishop of Canterbury, George Carey, knew the college well from his years as vicar of St Nic's Church in Durham's marketplace, and kindly agreed to be a patron, subsequently joined by Dr John Habgood, Archbishop of York and College Visitor. On his retirement halfway through the campaign, his successor Dr David Hope kindly agreed to become a patron in his stead.

The committee structure we adopted was recommended to us by our fundraising consultant, Iain Mulholland, who already knew the college well from its previous campaign in the 1980s when he had briefly acted as our fundraiser himself, and then trained up his successor. Iain was a rare individual, a man of real Christian commitment who understood both the complex worlds of the Church and of higher education, which are uniquely spanned by St John's. His professional support for the first months of this campaign was absolutely invaluable to this particular nervous inexperienced fundraiser. One of my personal sorrows in writing this book is that he sadly died before he knew of its existence. His likely wry humorous response exists in my imagination alone, but his influence still looms large through all that I have written.

Day-to-day direction of the campaign is carried out by a small executive committee, chaired by the campaign chairperson and comprising the four senior members of college staff, plus the staff of the development office. Monthly meetings are held, reviewing progress to date, discussing policy and giving the development office staff direction as to their immediate tasks and priorities. In addition a much broader group has been recruited, dubbed the Advisory Group, whose members have been selected to provide contact with a wide range of potential fundraising sources, or who had specific expertise to contribute. It is a slightly fluid body, with some members joining or leaving as their skills are needed for a particular phase of the campaign. We have kept our promise to seek not more than two full meetings a year from them, though many have given help and advice on a one-to-one basis on frequent occasions, by letter or telephone.

Our campaign has not lent itself as much as some to the use of volunteers, although certain patient individuals have keyed in addresses onto the database, stuffed envelopes, stuck on labels or assembled information packs with great patience from time to time. The student bodies of both Halls have lent a great deal of support in different ways, taking part enthusiastically in a number of special events, and acting as ambassadors for the campaign when necessary.

Points to remember

* Identify the key person to do the actual fundraising.

* Identify and recruit a chairperson or figurehead.

* Decide if you want patrons as well.

* Assemble a back-up team of advisers with expertise and/or contacts to share.

* Form a small executive committee to oversee the day-to-day running of the campaign.

* Enlist committed volunteers where there is a real job to be done.

* Don't forget the potential of all people with goodwill to help with specific jobs as the campaign proceeds.

---

4 Resources

If the procedures outlined so far seem daunting and beyond your reach, do not despair entirely, as there are sources of help available to you. These come in many forms: people, agencies, books, training courses and paid experts.

People

First of all, there will be a number of people with practical experience to help you along the way. Other organizations, churches or their leaders may have faced similar situations to your own. There is no point in reinventing the wheel and starting off from scratch if across the country there are even two or three others who have already been involved in fundraising for your type of project and who can offer real practical advice. If you don't know of any already, there may be others in your area who do. Those with regional or national church responsibilities may be best placed to come across helpful examples.

You may have contact already with others who have skills to share. Many church members will have picked up useful skills from their employment that could be put at your service. Some may work in areas that will be helpful to the project itself, which may reduce your costs. Anyone involved in marketing, design, financial management or the charitable sector generally would be able to make helpful suggestions and comments about aspects of your fundraising plans. If they are approached for help and like what you are planning to achieve, you may be able to recruit them as permanent volunteers.

Church records

Buried in cupboards in your vestry may be a wealth of information to help you. Churchwardens, PCC secretaries, treasurers and other church office bearers may also have wisdom and useful memories to offer, not to mention extra documentary evidence. You should be particularly interested in examining all available records if your church has ever done any fundraising before. Details of sources of past donations are invaluable. Each donation has a history to be unpicked: the people involved, their motivation for giving, who helped them to their decision, the sum involved, their address at the time. Those who already give regularly may be able to give a little more, perhaps managing a one-off extra gift if they feel your project is important enough. You will be able to trace other promising contacts, perhaps through wedding, baptism or funeral registers, articles in former parish magazines, etc. Have any celebrities or influential individuals ever visited or used the church for any reason? If so, they may remember their visit and be willing to do something practical to help you, if not initially to make a financial donation.

Directories and journals
It is only in the last ten years or so that fundraising as a recognized career has taken off on a substantial scale in Britain. Suddenly charities of every shape and size are looking to employ dedicated fundraising staff. Alongside this phenomenal growth have come an ever-increasing number of directories and journals designed to serve the expanding band of voluntary and professional fundraisers hungry for success.

Basic items on most fundraisers' shelves include major directories such as the *Directory of Grant Making Trusts*, now in two volumes and published regularly by the Charities Aid Foundation, and the wide range of directories produced by the Directory of Social Change. It would be quite easy to spend a three-figure sum after just your first inspection of what is available. If your resources are really tight, you might be able to get access to some of these through your local library, or to persuade a charity to let you visit their premises to browse through their copies. Be prepared for some in-depth researching, to identify sources of funding that have a close fit with the shape of your project. The choice is bewildering, so be ruthless in the criteria you use to identify possible sources. Remember that every other fundraiser in the land probably has these very same directories on a shelf next to their desk. As the number of applications submitted to trusts and companies inexorably rises, only those which fit all the criteria stand a chance of avoiding a rapid visit to the waste paper bin within minutes of arrival through the potential funder's letterbox.

Additional fruitful help might come from the growing number of regional directories, usually compiled by people based in your geographical area. A subscription to one or more of the fundraising journals – such as *Professional Fundraising*, *Trust Monitor*, *Corporate Citizen*, *Third Sector* – would offer up-to-date information about trends in giving, new sources, and new initiatives. It might just give you a head start on your rivals to scan their pages regularly. Again, if finance is a limiting factor, you might be able to find a local charity or agency willing to let you come in to study their copies. Fundraising to date remains a very helpful and companionable profession, and most professionals will do their best to help a small but genuine cause.

IT opportunities

Somewhere in your parish there is bound to be a computer buff, linked to the Internet, who can give you access to fundraising information on the World Wide Web. The number of websites and homepages out there which could be useful is literally growing daily. Much of the information at the time of writing emanates from the USA, which remains several years ahead of the UK in most things relating to the raising of money, but the UK influence is growing rapidly.

If you don't have access to the World Wide Web but can send and receive electronic mail (email) you may be able to subscribe to various discussion lists where fundraisers send regular messages into a general forum for discussion, usually seeking or offering help on very practical matters. A word of warning though – these lists are compelling reading, and can take up hours of time. The number of lists will again grow and grow as email becomes more widely available. There are also a number of helpful lists operating within the Church. Email has the advantage of being cheap and quick once you have made the initial investment in the necessary hardware and software. It is possible to mail a single message in seconds to thousands of subscribers, saving hundreds of pounds in postage, and allowing for near instantaneous replies. The fundraising implications of this very modern mode of communication are enormous, and grow daily.

Training courses, conferences

The growth of fundraising as a profession has also spawned a large number of training opportunities, as the number of consultants grows, and new trends develop. The cost and quality vary widely and it is well worth while asking around before putting in your order form. Personal recommendation of an effective course providing value for money from another fundraiser is one of the best ways to ensure your money is not wasted, at least until you know your way around the fundraising world. Although the fundraising sector has grown hugely in recent years, it is still true that many consultants and training providers know each other extremely well. Again, the Directory of Social Change are prominent in the field, providing a wide range of courses on aspects of fundraising and charity management, in various regions around the country, at a reasonable cost.

Local Institute of Charity Fundraising Managers (ICFM) groups often put on regular training days in the regions, which again provide good value for money, especially if you are located out of London. Several national conferences give an opportunity to enrol for a number of sessions on a range of useful topics within 48–72 hours. These include the Professional Fundraising Show and Charityfair in London in April and June respectively each year, and the National Fundraising Convention each July. Regional day conferences are often held around the country. Bursaries are sometimes available from local ICFM groups or ICFM nationally for their own training events and it is well worth enquiring about these if you take out membership. There is often almost as much benefit to be derived from rubbing shoulders with your fellow fundraisers and networking with them as from the content of the sessions themselves. Horizons are widened and enthusiasm rekindled through sharing with others who face the same challenges and concerns.

Statutory funds
Certain kinds of church project may be eligible for statutory funds of different kinds. This depends on the nature and to some extent the geographical location of the project. No statutory source of funding is likely to support any project whose primary *raison d'être* appears to be evangelization or the seeking of converts. However, if you are in an area of rural or urban deprivation and if your project will bring substantial benefit for the community, you may find that you are eligible for consideration e.g. for money from the Single Regeneration Budget or the European Union. Agencies such as your local Council for Voluntary Service or Rural Community Council, the Economic Development Unit in you local council or the local government office may be

able to advise. The Inner Cities Religious Council was set up by the Department of the Environment in London a few years ago to help 'faith communities', i.e. groups of believers from different faiths in Britain, to access statutory sources of funding.

Professional help

Some churches and many charities have gone down the route of engaging a professional fundraising consultant to actually direct their fundraising activities, bypassing the need for their own fundraiser. Most have found that though this may represent a substantial outlay in the short term, this investment has reaped dividends in a focused, well-planned and efficiently executed campaign that has yielded maximum income with minimum time and energy. Personal recommendation from other churches is probably the most useful factor to bear in mind here – not all fundraisers, however good, will have experiences of the particular challenge of fundraising in a Christian context, and appreciate the nuances and subtleties of church life. In general, membership of the ICFM is a good indication of professional competence and ability. The ICFM publish a useful yearbook giving a wide range of information of different services to charities, and include a list of recognized consultants, together with an indication of their areas of expertise.

ICFM regional groups

As well as providing national support and training for fundraisers, there are a number of ICFM regional groups covering the country, and it is well worth while making contact with your nearest group to find out what activities they offer. Many will have regular informal meetings, perhaps with a speaker or a discussion focused on a particular area of interest, to which all involved in fundraising are welcome, and where you will meet many other fundraisers with expertise to share. Such meetings can give real insights into the fundraising possibilities on your doorstep, and can sometimes alert you to pitfalls to avoid.

College example: The resources we used

On beginning my work for the St John's development campaign, I was helped enormously by the very full and complete records bequeathed to me by a previous fundraiser, also a former student of the college, who was involved in the college's last major fundraising effort in the 1980s. The records enabled me to trace who had been approached in the past, and who had given or refused. It was especially helpful to read through the actual correspondence involved. There was no mystique here, no hidden key to success; just a lot of very hard work, systematically and meticulously prepared. I came to believe that I too in my turn would be able to write such letters and see some of the same results.

I count myself particularly fortunate to work for an institution that thoroughly understands the needs for adequate education for the task in hand. Through my work I have come across other fundraisers across the voluntary sector who have had to fight for every penny expended on training, and whose ability to do their job has been severely curtailed through lack of investment in helping them to work more professionally. I've always been grateful that St John's has understood the need for its campaign staff to receive good training. I suppose the knowledge that they were employing a complete novice as their fundraiser provided some basic motivation!

Building up a library of directories was one of the first tasks; we began by purchasing our own copies of the main Charities Aid Foundation and Directory of Social Change directories. It is now possible to search for trusts through computer programs such as '*Funderfinder*', but I have always preferred to do my own detailed research, getting a feel for each trust through detailed examination of the causes it supports and the people involved. I'm sure I wouldn't absorb half as much information if a computer carried out this process for me. Other publications have followed: trust directories local to the North-East, directories of local and multinational companies, DIY guides to various aspects of fundraising, subscriptions to some of the main fundraising periodicals. As many of our former students are ordained Anglican clergy, I am also probably one of the few people to painstakingly read the entire contents of *Crockford's Clerical Directory* from cover to cover, thus detecting many more of our former students who had lost touch with us since their time in Durham. I earnestly hope that most of them have been pleased to hear from us again!

Training in the form of seminars and courses has been the other important component that has helped me gain some competence in fundraising and to avoid many mistakes. Taking out membership of the ICFM and participating in their foundation course for fundraisers was a great help, both in terms of the knowledge imparted and the networks of fellow fundraisers it has allowed me to tap into, nationally and regionally. On the whole I have found that conferences covering a range of topics in a concentrated space of time have provided good value for money, even taking the trainfare to London from the North-East into account. I have been fortunate to attend the National Fundraisers Convention, held in the Midlands every year under the auspices of the ICFM, giving me the opportunity to rub shoulders with the big names of the profession.

Points to remember

* Look for contacts among the people who surround you.

* Research past supporters from your existing records.

* Scour the directories publicly available.

* Surf the Internet.

* Invest in some training.

* Consult local and national agencies.

* Consider hiring a professional consultant.

---

5 The case

Having discussed the institution's vision and mission in general terms, and identified a sound project for which the church wishes to seek funds, the time has come to think about material that can be used for specific applications.

By now you should know the broad shape of the project you are putting forward, be sure that your project meets a real need, and have done some hard thinking about the background information that will help you make a case to potential supporters when you write your application. Your supporters should share your vision and be committed to it themselves. The time has come to hone this material in order to help funders share your conviction that your project is more important than all the other charitable causes they are presented with daily.

Unique Selling Points (USPs)

This phrase is taken from the world of marketing, where sellers of various products have learned to assess the items they have for sale, identifying what makes them stand out in the marketplace from all their competitors. There are parallels with your situation as you go out to 'sell' your cause to funders. They are inevitably faced with a large array of potential projects to fund, and need to know what is special, what is different about your organization, church or project.

Uniqueness can lie in the essence of your institution, in the distinctiveness of your ministry, or in the innovative way you are seeking to provide a solution to an obvious need. Yet again, it is worth discussing exhaustively amongst members and supporters just what it is that makes your project or cause special. Funders really have to know why they should give to you rather than other good causes.

Uniqueness can also lie in the issue you are seeking to address, or the problem you are seeking to solve, and in the number or type of beneficiaries. The statistics you assembled as a result of the last chapter can be very useful here. They can underline the need you are meeting, your measured and planned approach to the problem, and highlight your likely effectiveness in delivering a solution as a result of donations received.

Facts, figures and statistics

Use of reliable statistics will give a businesslike impression of your activities and will demonstrate how carefully you have researched the need you are meeting and the nature of the solution you have come up with. You may not use all the information at any one time to any one donor. However, to know that you have done your research and have a full armoury of facts and figures at your disposal will only strengthen your own confidence, and can enable you to give a speedy and authoritative answer to the random questions that potential donors may put to you at any time.

Many useful statistics about the area in which you operate will be available from the local council. Other more detailed and extremely useful demographic information can be culled from the returns of the last census. This can often add powerful illustrations about the particular social needs of the area; for example a low level of car ownership and the number of outside toilets still in use are two common indicators of poverty, while a higher than average number of single-parent households or frail elderly may demonstrate needs of a different kind. Crime statistics are another source of powerful argument that people in your area are seriously disadvantaged.

Local knowledge and common sense can sometimes identify other significant factors. If large areas of a town were bulldozed in the 1960s and replaced with council estates and high-rise blocks on the edges of the community, the chances are that family life between the generations has been fractured and that there is a weaker sense of community. If a new road has been built through an area, providing an artificial barrier between former neighbours, those living on one side of the road may have been marginalized and have fewer facilities than those on the other. In a rural context, if a railway station has been closed or a bus service withdrawn, those without cars will experience much greater isolation.

Along with the social critique of your area can go a list of the different agencies operating in the community and the kind of help they are able to provide, quoting rough numbers of beneficiaries if possible. Pay particular attention to any agencies or churches appearing to duplicate the service your project will be providing. Will you be serving two different constituencies? Have you any plans for effective partnership? Is your project clearly needed in addition to the existing one? Can you demonstrate a basic groundswell of local support for your plans, or quote individual instances (protecting identities where appropriate) of people who will be significantly helped?

Maps, building plans, diagrams, graphs, bar charts, pie charts and photographs may all have their place in your range of supporting evidence. A file of letters of support for your cause can be compiled. Local councillors, the MP, MEP, leader of the council, mayor, lord lieutenant of the county, local aristocracy, local community leaders and church leaders of all denominations may all be willing to put pen to paper to support you. Some may be grateful if you actually draft the letter for them to sign! If they are not willing for any reason to write a letter, they may instead be willing to discuss a sentence or two quoting their views (these should only be reprinted with permission, of course). Even a single phrase endorsing your work, which can be incorporated later into your literature or strategically dropped into your application or covering letter, will add credibility to your cause.

Drafting and producing literature

The written word often has a key part to play in giving an impression about you and your project. Unlike the spoken word it can be carefully planned and edited, and may remain as a semi-permanent record of your approach style for months or years. It can reach a great variety of people over time and if done well can create an initial positive image of your church and project in the minds of all who read it.

It is therefore worth investing some money in good supporting literature. This does not need to involve vast sums, especially if you have access to a word processor, and someone who knows how to use it to its full capacity, experimenting with different fonts, point sizes (i.e. the size of the type used) and layouts to get the presentation as professional as possible. Two sides of A4, possibly folded into an A5 leaflet, can be produced at home on a straightforward PC and printer, and folded by hand, without necessarily incurring any professional printing costs at all. Alternatively, a local printer, if convinced of your cause, may offer cut price rates, perhaps in return for a line or two of recognition of his 'gift in kind'.

It may be useful to draft a variety of different documents which outline different aspects of your project, and which act as a pool of material to been drawn upon as and when needed to back up your real applications to funders. Background history, statistical reports, case histories of beneficiaries, methods of giving and your overall strategy may all be reduced to A4 summary sheets. If you have access to a scanner and a colour printer, these can even reproduce photographs to an acceptable standard, greatly increasing the range of material you can satisfactorily produce 'in house'. It helps if all your documents match in presentation, and appear to be one of a coherent set. If your church already has a logo or specially designed headed notepaper, the logo or heading could be reproduced at the top, and the typeface chosen to echo it.

If the project is a major one, and a professionally designed printed brochure is deemed to be appropriate, once again much thought should go into the text and presentation. It is very easy to spend a great deal of money on glossy brochures that may not do the job you wish them to. If you have any links with other churches or organizations that have been fundraising recently, it could be very informative to obtain copies of their brochures, to get a sense of the possibilities and of what to your mind seems to work and what doesn't. You may well find that many in the congregation are already receiving direct mail from a variety of charities; ask your members to save all their 'junk mail' for a few weeks, then gather it together and search for principles in layout or design which might work for you (of course without infringing copyright). Seeing how the professionals have gone about it may help you avoid missing out some vital component, such as a contact name and address so those who are impressed with what you have written know how to get in touch with you.

One possible approach is to go for a simple commercially produced brochure which provides all the basic information about your project, with a flap inside the back cover into which can be slotted extra supporting documents as relevant. You will find that trusts and other funders vary enormously as to the amount of information about you that they require. To send everything to everyone is costly and will only annoy those who ask for a simple application. This method combines professionalism with flexibility.

Role-play

It can be an extremely useful exercise to engage in a little role-play in preparation for the real-life occasions when you will have to commend your project to potential funders. One exercise which can throw up obvious questions to which you have not yet found the right answers is to run the arguments you have put together to support your case, and copies of any draft literature, in front of as many people as possible who are unfamiliar with your work. Sometimes you can be so close to a cause that is dear to your heart that you cease to see it through objective eyes, and assume that everyone already has a background knowledge or understands the underlying needs. Strangers to your work can sometimes highlight basic information that you have omitted.

Another way to practise your approaches and to ensure that you know your material inside out is to take turns within your team to act out being in a fundraising situation. The person playing the funder can try to ask as many awkward questions as possible, while the fundraiser tries to answer them smoothly and confidently, without drying up or being lost for words. Having run through a situation like this in role-play can add much greater confidence when the situation is for real. An added benefit is that the fundraising team will learn to speak as one voice, sharing the same emphases, and conveying a consistent message to all enquirers.

College example: The campaign brochure

St John's College decided at an early stage that a major development campaign warranted a substantial investment in an attractive brochure, carefully thought out and produced to a professional standard. Negotiations were begun with a local graphic design firm, who had an excellent reputation for good work, and who had a particular sympathy for projects with a Christian basis. This company tendered for the work alongside a couple of other companies, and were subsequently officially engaged to take on the task. Their enthusiasm for the campaign was such that they agreed to charge a lower rate as part of their own charitable ethos as a company.

Initial discussions focused around the ethos and image of the college. The title – 'Sharing the vision' – was selected, as both encapsulating what the college was about, and as lending continuity, following on in sequence from an earlier successful campaign run by the college in the 1980s, which had taken 'Vision for tomorrow' as its slogan.

The concept of the college as a place of open doors – sending students out to serve the Church and the world, but also welcoming people in – became central to the brochure. A picture of the solid wooden doors of the college's main entrance, held enticingly ajar, with a glow of warm attractive golden light issuing forth, was selected for the front cover, and in a nice design touch, the door image was repeated on each subsequent page, miniaturized down and used in the margin as a background to the page number.

A number of photographs were commissioned to give light and colour to the brochure; these were eventually produced in two short sessions from a professional photographer to ensure the quality and angles were just right. Meanwhile, the principal began work on the basic text, using basic headings: a foreword, what is a college, what makes St John's unique, achievement, extension, from vision to substance, how you can contribute to the campaign. This led to eight pages of A4 text within a cover. A flap was built into the back cover, allowing further A4 sheets to be tucked in, and a series of information sheets, one for each project, were designed to complement the brochure.

The information sheets were produced in a style which echoed that of the brochure, but which could also be used alone, when applications were being made to small donors with a specific interest in just one project. The brochure, and each individual sheet, included the college's address, phone and fax numbers. The charitable status of the college was highlighted and the company number given. St John's College, in common with some other educational institutions is an 'exempt charity', and thus does not have a charity registration number to quote. However, under the 1993 Charities Act it is now a legal requirement that a registration number, where one exists, should be included by charities on all their literature, including letterhead.

Modern computer technology allowed a great deal of playing around with the format in the later design stages. Photos could be repositioned, enlarged or diminished, faded into the background with a watermark effect, superimposed on each other. Fonts, style and point sizes and the tint of the background paper were discussed *ad infinitum*. Several times the design company came up with a version that the college felt was almost there but not quite, and were asked to come back again with further versions. At last all were happy with what had been achieved.

The cost of the brochure and all the information sheets, even given the generous discount given by the company, was substantial. However, when broken down into thirteen for each of the different projects, and divided again to cover the five years of the campaign, the investment has not seemed disproportionate. Careful thought in the early stages has meant that as the campaign reaches its final stages the brochure is still fresh, relevant and eminently usable. Donors and supporters alike have complimented the college on its quality. A few donors have felt that the quality has indicated an over-generous amount of expenditure, but most have understood our reasons for such an investment when our reasons have been explained to them. Major donors have found the brochure completely acceptable.

Points to remember

* Identify all the things that make your organization and your project unique.

* Use other people's research where you can.

* Present your statistics attractively – use visual methods where possible.

* Get people to write letters in support, or supply usable quotes endorsing your work.

* Put enough thought into your campaign literature.

* Produce a variety of short background documents ready to back up your main application.

* Indulge in a little role-play – make sure all the team know your case for funding inside-out.

---

6 Targeting applications

Do your sums!

The time has come to do a little thinking about where exactly the money you need is likely to come from, and how to target your applications to the sources most likely to supply the funding you need.

But first a final comment about the costings for your project. It is vitally important that these are accurate. You should have reliable estimates for the costs of every aspect of your project, and make sure that nothing has been left out. In addition it is legitimate to include the hidden costs to your church or institution of running the project – extra staff time, photocopying, telephone, and other administrative costs, as long as you make it clear what you are doing, and that you are not just plucking figures out of the air. It is also legitimate to include the costs of actually raising the money – again the time involved and the administrative costs. Remember to add VAT where relevant. Beware – if you pitch your first total too low, it will be far harder to raise the extra amount needed at the end of the project.

Up to and including this point, it is possible to introduce major refinements, and to scale the project up or down significantly, without compromising the image funders will have of you as people who know what they are doing and who have done their homework adequately. A cool head is needed to assess whether the money is actually out there for the kind of project you are hoping to fund.

Pareto Effect

Once you have a firm financial target in mind, you can go on to look seriously at where the money might come from.

Purely in terms of the types of sum that come in, you are almost bound to find that the 'Pareto Effect' comes into operation. Time and again this simple mathematical equation seems to hold good; that around 80 per cent of the funding you need will come from just 20 per cent of the sources who give to you, and conversely that the remaining 80 per cent of donors will give smaller sums to make up the final 20 per cent of your total. In cash terms, if you are looking to raise £100,000 then £80,000 of it will come from comparatively few sources, whereas the final £20,000 is likely to come from a far higher number of donors giving many smaller donations.

Faced with this seemingly inexorable law of modern fundraising, many fundraisers decide to expend most of their energies pursuing the few donor possibilities capable of giving substantial amounts as their priority. Certainly, when there is only one fundraiser in operation and resources are limited, some strategic targeting of your time and energies seems to be only common sense.

Success breeds success

Another reason for focusing your energies very specifically on just a few sources of funding in the early stages of your campaign is that it can be particularly difficult to attract the first major donation to a good cause. Special efforts are often required to obtain these 'lead gifts'. Once you have secured one or two major gifts, another unwritten rule of fundraising can come into play: that success certainly seems to breed further success. Many fundraising campaigns thus build in a substantial 'secret' or 'silent' phase to their activities, strictly limiting the number of people who know that any fundraising is going on at all. Their aim is to secure at least one major donation before making any public announcement about their fundraising plans. Some campaigns have even sought to raise half their total before announcing to the world at large that they are in business.

There are several advantages to this approach. Meticulous planning can go on in the early stages without public expectation of quick success. The first approaches to funders can be highly focused and concentrated without the distractions of all the other lesser kinds of fundraising activity – events, media coverage, and swathes of smaller applications going out. The transition from secret phase to public phase can then be accompanied by as big a splash in the media as you can muster, communicating to the public and the local community that this is a successful project, already on the way to completion. Subsequently other smaller donors will be encouraged to give, knowing that substantial donors considered your project worthy of support and that they can therefore rest assured that smaller gifts will also be well used.

Donor matrices

Some fundraisers have found it helpful to sit down and make a table of the types of sum that they need to attract, taking the Pareto Effect into account, and then to match this up with a second table showing sources of funding capable of coming up with the necessary levels of gift. According to this approach, and using a campaign for £100,000 as a model, the scale of gifts needed might look something like this:

1	×	25,000	=	25,000
2	×	10,000	=	20,000
5	×	5,000	=	25,000
10	×	1,000	=	10,000
20	×	500	=	10,000
25	×	100	=	2,500
50	×	50	=	2,500
100	×	25	=	2,500
250	×	10	=	2,500

In order to achieve this kind of response, the fundraiser needs to identify four or five realistic sources of funding who might be able to give sums in the region of £25,000, and a further 10–15 sources who might give £10,000. Below this, perhaps 30–40 sources capable of giving £1,000–£5,000 need to be identified. This will allow you to have a number of the inevitable refusals, but will increase the probability that somewhere along the line you may get a 'yes'.

Using contacts

If you have a contact of any sort with a potential donor, the chances that you will eventually secure a donation immediately become far more favourable. Every source of funding that is publicly known about these days receives far more applications for funds than can ever be responded to. At the very least, your contact may be able to get your application given serious consideration rather than have it take a short route from the letterbox to the bin because of the sheer volume of applications you are competing with. If a potential funder can actually be persuaded to visit you to see what you are doing, you are much more likely to receive a gift of some kind, assuming that your project has any merit at all.

Your supporters will have far more moral power to persuade their contacts to give if they have already dug deep into their own pockets to make a personal donation themselves. If they are happy to have this fact made known in the process of cultivating a potential donor they are in a much stronger psychological position to ask. The person being approached will know that your supporters think enough of what you are trying to achieve to give not only their time but also their money to see it become reality.

When trying to identify people who might be happy to be used as intermediaries, it is possible to use two different approaches. One is to work from the top down – to look in directories of philanthropists, trusts and companies for sources of funds which are capable of giving the sort of sum you are looking for. Then try to find links with them that may predispose them to consider your request seriously, and ultimately to give to you rather than to the many others who will also be approaching them. They may originate from your area, give to similar projects already, know one of your contacts and respect their views, or have another personal reason for being interested.

The second approach is to look at the people and contacts you already have, and to work from the bottom up. Look at the individuals who give to you already, or those who are personally known to people within your church or organization. Local landowners, aristocracy, business moguls, politicians may all be able to open doors for you. They may know trustees of trusts, directors of companies or mix socially with those who have the capacity to give large sums. Remember that practical help in opening doors or raising the profile of your cause can be more important in the long run than a small personal cheque – though the ideal is to secure both!

People may be candidates to act as contacts for you for a number of different reasons, and the more research you are able to undertake, the more links you may be able to establish. Local history may tell you if any celebrities have personal or family links with your geographical area; they may have gone to school in your town, or have grown up close by. They may have a strong personal interest in an aspect of your campaign. For example, does it bring benefit to young people in the community? ... the homeless or unemployed? Are they keen on church music or bell-ringing, if the fundraising is for your organ or bell tower? Are they committed Christians themselves?

Strategy documents

Supporters of your cause and donors can be encouraged to see the target you are seeking to raise as realistic if you produce a strategy document, outlining what you need to raise, where different proportions of this money might be found, and how you intend to go about actually raising funds from each kind of source. Breaking down a large sum into smaller amounts like this can make it all seem far more achievable to onlookers, showing that you have thought your strategy through properly. Different sources of potential funding can sometimes be helpfully broken down even further, e.g. by suggesting how many trusts might be expected to give certain amounts, and how many new covenants might be needed from individual supporters. Mention of a timescale can help too, so that supporters don't feel the campaign will stretch on and on into the foreseeable future.

Avoid 'vaccinations'

Part of the reason to go to all the trouble of identifying a range of donors who might be capable of giving different amounts is to make sure that you maximize their opportunity to give to you. If you ask for too much a trust can dismiss your application out of hand, feeling that the small amount they may have to give will make little difference to the scale of your needs. Alternatively if you ask for too little, you are likely to get a small amount from a source which might have been capable of being one of your major donors. Several large trusts have a system of fast-track small donations, although they may be able on occasion to give five- or six-figure sums. Receipt of a small donation may preclude you from going back to ask for a larger sum for a period of time, if ever. Your targeted source of funding has become desensitized to further appeals from you. Sometimes a cheque for a thousand pounds from trusts like these can actually be deeply disappointing.

College example: Strategy

The St John's College campaign began with a low-key 'private' focus, seeking a substantial donation from a trust that had supported us generously in the past. The donation we eventually received was worth a tenth of our target total. Securing this demonstrated to all and sundry that we meant business as we announced our plans to the world at large. Significantly, the trust gave part of this donation in the form of a pledge, which would be released to us when we found another donor to 'match' it – a powerful lever to present to other funders.

We then held two public launches for the campaign, one in the North-East and one in London, and spent the next few months following up all the leads that came from the personal contacts we made at these events. This period of frenetic activity then led to a time of reassessment and consolidation, and a strategy document was produced to help focus our efforts for the remaining years of the campaign.

This document outlined the objectives of the campaign (£1.2 million raised within four years for 13 distinct projects, and the establishment of a committed base of donors for the future) and the methods that would be used to achieve this objective. It described the structure of the development office directed by an executive committee and supported by an advisory group. It looked at realistic sources of funding for the balance that still needed to be raised (at that time some £900,000), and outlined a timetable for approaches to these varied sources.

Points to remember

* Calculate exactly how much you need.

* Be able to justify all your figures.

* Remember the Pareto Effect.

* Build up donor matrices for each category of potential donor .

* Channel your energies to major gifts first.

* Formulate a coherent overall strategy.

* Make sure you ask donors for enough!

---

7 Writing applications

Consider the recipient

You may feel that you now have all the information you need to write a stunning application that would melt the heart of the most miserly soul in the land. However, you are still not ready to put pen to paper. The next task is to find out all you can about the people you are writing to. Companies often publish details of their charitable giving in their annual reports; it can be useful to give them a ring and ask for a copy. The larger trusts likewise often publish material about their giving, which can give useful hints about the type of project they like to support. It may also help you choose what level of donation to ask for. Through other contacts in the fundraising world locally you may know some of the likes, dislikes and foibles of some of the funders in your region.

Many donors have common concerns when looking through the applications they receive and deciding which ones will be successful. They will look for projects that fit their policy. They will look for value for money – are you offering a good deal in your attempt to spend their money for them, or do other people seem to achieve better results for less cash? Do you have a track record of delivering what you promise, and a good reputation locally? Are you in a sound financial state yourself? Are the costings accurate, or are you likely to need to come back to them for more money in the near future? Will you publicize their donation? (N.B. according to the donor, this could be a good or bad point; always clear any publicity about the gift with them first.)

Follow the guidelines

It cannot be stressed highly enough that you should follow any advice given in published guidelines to the letter. If a telephone number is given and you are encouraged to ring first to discuss your application, you can only benefit from doing this. However, if they publicly discourage such calls, don't do it! Most sources of funding have some published guidelines to help you; use them. If they say they don't fund individuals, don't apply on behalf of a needy person in the church, however strongly you feel on their behalf. If they say they don't fund building work, don't apply for your new church hall. If they look like the ideal trust, but their beneficial area is London and the South-East, don't apply for a grant for Carlisle. To ignore their guidelines when you apply amounts to saying 'I haven't bothered to do my research first' – hardly the best way to commend yourself to them in your first contact.

Presentation

These days it is important that your application looks good as well as being well thought out and put together. The days of handwritten pencilled applications on grubby dog-eared paper are gone for most trusts. Neat legible applications are the order of the day. It is important that they are suitable to be clearly photocopied for inward distribution once at the trust or company. This will probably mean typing the application – making a couple of carbon copies for your own records – and if possible wordprocessing it. You can play around with the page size, font and point size to produce a format that looks businesslike and uncluttered, and produce a respectable result on plain white A4 paper without spending a fortune.

Format

The format should be clear and easy to follow. I usually give the application a title, incorporating the name of the donor to whom I am applying, followed by the title of the project. I then describe aspects of the project in various succeeding paragraphs, each with a separate heading. The first paragraph is always a simple two or three sentence summary of the project including the amount being applied for. This helps the trust's own administrators to know what the project is about without having to wade through lines of text to find out for themselves. Many trusts routinely write their own brief summaries for possible recipients of grants anyway as part of their normal procedure; doing this for them may create goodwill by saving them a job. It also means that you remain in control of exactly what goes into it!

Other paragraphs may cover such areas as a description of the church or institution, the work you are already doing, the immediate background to the project, the need which the project will address, how you propose to meet this need, the benefits that will flow from it, the numbers of people who will benefit, precise costings, and how the project will run once it has been funded. Introduce your 'unique selling points' and statistics to back up your descriptions wherever relevant. Clarity and concise use of words are vital at every stage. Your first draft should be edited and revised to say all that you want to say with the minimum of waffle or verbal padding.

Always be positive

After devising the first draft of an application, it can make a real difference to run through your text seeking to be positive in all the language you use. Make sure that if you paint the needs and problems you are facing as very black, you also make it clear that you are offering real practical solutions, and that the money you raise will make a qualitative difference. Highlight your past successes. Don't be apologetic if the project seems to be just a small drop in the ocean compared to the needs; focus on what you know you can achieve, and treat the rest as a further challenge for the future.

Many donors don't see themselves as pouring money into a bottomless pit of need, but like to see their activities as investments for the good of society in whatever field they operate. Remember that those who invest usually keep an eye open for the level of return on their investment. The more their money is likely to achieve the more likely they will be to give. Spell out not only the direct effects their donation will have, but any knock-on benefits that you can see as well. Your application should also include a description of how you will measure the benefits that will flow from your project, which will give extra credence to your claims.

Appendices

Your formal application should be as concise as possible, certainly no more than three sides of A4 and just one if possible, especially for smaller trusts. However, judicious use of appendices can help convey further information. For example, any feasibility study produced at an earlier stage of the planning could be attached. Basic costings can be broken down and elaborated upon in a further sheet of A4; architects drawings and plans, even photographs can be attached to give a more vivid image of your building project; and copies of the annual accounts for your church or charity can be enclosed to give a fair idea of the health of your overall finances to potential funders. Basic accounts can be backed up by a copy of your business plan for the first few years of operations of your project, to help funders see that you have approached the whole thing in a businesslike fashion.

Another possibility is to draw up two or three brief case studies based on fact, used with the permission of those involved; these could illustrate the human value of what you are trying to do. If you are writing several applications at once to different funders, check each application individually before you put them in the post, to be absolutely sure that you have included the information they specifically ask for. Beware of deluging the smaller trusts with too much paperwork; they will not have the resources to deal with it. It may be enough to send an application on a couple of sides of A4, but to let them know what further appendices and information are readily available, should they require it.

Covering letters

The reception your application receives may be helped by the impression you are able to convey in your covering letter. This should be concise and polite. It should comprise three to four paragraphs, fitting into a page of A4 with ease, unless you have a particular reason to be more expansive. It can contain anything you wish the secretary or correspondent of the trust to know which doesn't necessarily need to be part of the formal application, and is an opportunity to offer to be available to answer further questions and supply information if necessary. If you do have a contact with any of the trustees, or have been encouraged by someone with a connection to the trust to make your application, it is courteous to let the correspondent know.

Double-check and check again before you send it!

Watch out for little slips and errors before anything goes in the post. Are names spelt correctly at the head of the letter, in the salutation you use and on the envelope? If you have been producing several applications on a word processor in close succession, have you made all the right changes to personalize them? If you get tired or are under time pressure it is easy to make little slips like these, which appear as appalling large blunders to the person at the other end who actually opens your application. Always read through letters that have been typed up by volunteers before signing them. Finally, it can be useful yet again to find a willing friend or relative who knows nothing about your work and ask them to skim through a sample application. If they feel that you are using jargon, or don't understand what you are trying to achieve and why, think seriously about redrafting in plainer English. Remember that many trusts have so many applications to consider that they only have time to skim through quickly. A concise, direct and simple approach will be much appreciated by the recipient.

College example: A real application to major charitable trusts for the Outdoor Activities Centre

Application by St John's College Durham to the XYZ Charitable Trust: Outdoor Activities Centre

Summary
To extend and modernize No 23 North Bailey, an 18th century listed grade 2 building in the heart of Durham's ancient city centre, to form a self-catering residential centre with fire certificate for up to 30 residents plus 4 leaders.

Background
St John's College is a unique educational establishment, combining under one roof both St John's Hall (some 330 undergraduates and postgraduates studying the whole range of academic courses available in the University of Durham), and Cranmer Hall (some 100 men and women preparing for full-time Christian ministry). It has an evangelical Christian foundation, and all tutorial staff of both Halls are committed Christians. The College is currently engaged upon a major Development Campaign, seeking to raise £1.2 million within five years for thirteen diverse projects. It has received just over half a million pounds to date, and several of the projects will be getting under way. A brochure outlining the aims and objectives of the Campaign is included as Appendix A.

Why an Outdoor Activities Centre?
St John's College occupies a site on the ancient peninsula of

Durham with grounds sloping down to the River Wear, which
provides an ideal stretch of water for elementary canoeing
instruction, while just a few hundred yards further along
there is a six-mile stretch of water running down to Finchale
Priory for more advanced training. There is currently no
other self-catering accommodation for this kind of group within
the city.

The College has a strong tradition of community involvement,
stretching back through the decades, and flowing from its
distinctive Christian ethos. Its students are involved in a
number of `pastoralia' projects every year, many including work
with children. Many undergraduates apply to St John's because
they wish to engage in voluntary work alongside their degree
studies. The College in turn wishes to provide an environment
where young people have many opportunities for personal growth
and development in more areas than academic achievement alone.
There is a need for ordinands too to have the opportunity to
learn basic skills through involvement in the life of a centre
like this. Such experiences will be carried forward into their
future work and ministry in the Church. This project also aims
to mend the sometimes acrimonious relationships in existence
between `town' and `gown' in Durham, by providing a pattern for
harmonious and mutually satisfying involvement.

The Development Campaign currently being taken forward by St
John's College seeks to make St John's a place of open doors.
We envisage that there may be some overlap between local young
people receiving employment training and communication skills
through courses at our `Cross Gate Centre' ten minutes' walk
away and the natural clientele for the Outdoor Activities
Centre. This project forms a key part of our overall strategy
to become a resource for the community in which we are set.
More details about it are laid out on the Outdoor Activities
Centre information sheet labelled Appendix B.

The Building
23 North Bailey has been in the possession of the College since
the 1950s, and is currently used for student accommodation in
University term-time. It stands apart from the rest of the
College's property, and lies in the shadow of Durham's ancient

cathedral in the heart of the city. The gardens at the back overlook the River Wear, and include a track down to the water- side. 23 North Bailey is already used for holidays run by students for young people in vacations, although it is patently unsuitable for this purpose, having no facilities for cooking, communal eating or meeting rooms. Our experience in running a conference trade using our other buildings has shown that there is undoubtedly a demand for cheap self-catering accommodation of this kind, which is not being met at present. Consultation with architects has led to a scheme reordering the existing building internally, providing a self-catering kitchen, drying facilities, a leaders' lounge and a dining room on the ground floor, an extra double bedroom and utility area on the first floor, and building a small extension and storage area to the rear which will function as a games room/residents' lounge, and provide space for storage of canoes etc. This extension will allow the Centre to function for non-residential training courses even during University term-time.

Plans of 23 North Bailey are included as Appendix C.

The Beneficiaries
In addition to existing student-led initiatives such as Durham Youth Camp and the Northern Ireland Youth Encounter, there is evidence of widespread interest in our plans from external potential users. Some schools, churches and youth groups will wish to bring their own leaders and organize their use of time and facilities themselves. Others may wish to make use of the close links established by the College with Outdoor Adventure Development Ministries, whose director is a qualified leader and trainer, and who is a former student of the College. This organization is willing to provide training to students of the College so that they can themselves provide a pool of qualified helpers to support visiting groups. Excerpts from a first draft of a recently commissioned Feasibility Study for the Centre are included as Appendix D.

A selection of letters in support of the Outdoor Activities Centre is included as Appendix E.

Projected Use

In the first year of operation the following take-up of the Outdoor Activities Centre is projected:

existing student-led camps to continue	40 youngsters participating
10 new groups to be accommodated	150 youngsters participating
Students to be trained as canoe instructors	10
Leaders from youth groups to be trained	10
Total beneficiaries in year one	210

In addition we hope to foster links with the College's Urban Mission Centre in Gateshead, providing training and facilities for a number of young people growing up in a deprived inner city environment there.

The Cost

The total cost to extend and modernize 23 North Bailey fully will be in the region of £80,000, with a further £14,000 expenditure to equip the kitchen and drying room and the games room, and to purchase bunk beds and bedding. Costs for canoes and other activities equipment have been estimated at just under £9,000. Total expenditure therefore stands at over £100,000.

More detailed costings are available as Appendix F.

Once established, the running costs of the Centre will be absorbed into the overall College budget for buildings. Income derived from bookings will cover staff costs and depreciation of equipment.

The College has to date received £X towards this scheme, from a range of donors including ... Further pledges totalling £X have been made by two other trusts. £X has been spent to date on a Feasibility Study looking at all aspects of the Centre's management, administration and functions. The sum raised to date thus totals £X.

PLANNING

The College therefore needs to raise a further £X for building costs, and a subsequent £X in equipment for the Centre to allow for the full range of activities. We would therefore be grateful if the Trustees could consider a major contribution towards the £X shortfall needed to extend and modernize 23 North Bailey over the summer of XXXX. We look forward to hearing their response.

Mrs Jane Grieve

Development Director

Points to remember

* Treat each recipient of an application as an individual.

* Double-check the trust entries and insights from your contacts.

* Spend time on presentation; make it clear and logical.

* Always present facts in a positive light.

* Think through what appendices to send – if any.

* Use your covering letter as another opportunity to impress.

* Check it for comments with someone who knows nothing about your work.

8 Types of gift

Straight cash

Always useful! The simplest and easiest method for most people to give; it can come in the form of actual coins and notes if the gift is made in person. However, most people with the means to make more than the smallest donations will be likely to have a cheque book and may prefer to give by cheque. Larger charities often have the facility to receive gifts by credit card; however, most small churches and charities would not have the resources to receive donations in this form. Whether churches would increase their giving by offering this facility is an interesting point.

It is important that a good system is in place for receiving and counting cash income, whether it comes on the regular Sunday collection plate, is handed over personally or arrives through the letterbox. Gifts in cash form are the most vulnerable to fraud or theft. No one person should have sole access to the money at any one time, nor should it be left unattended in vestries or church offices. It is important that there are regular opportunities to bank cash income, both for security reasons and in order to place the money at the Church's disposal quickly.

Deeds of covenant

Covenanted income has two distinct advantages: it allows a donor's gift to be augmented by claiming back the tax the donor has already paid on this money from the Inland Revenue, and it allows the organization to be fairly confident of an income stream that will continue over the years through the lifetime of the covenant. Many churches will have a covenant secretary, and be familiar with this form of giving. Donors pledge a certain level of regular giving over a four-year period, specifying an amount *per annum*, and whether they wish to pay this in monthly, quarterly or annual instalments.

The proportion of a church's income made up of covenanted giving can vary widely. Sometimes there are few taxpayers in the congregation, and a comparatively low proportion may be all that is possible. However, churches should pay attention to maximizing giving from this source. It often needs months of patient and tactful 'selling' to gain a wide take-up. Many people may have basic misapprehensions about the whole principle, worrying about taking on a commitment for four years ahead when their circumstances are uncertain. They may feel that giving should be entirely secret. Wives with no income of their own may be in a sensitive situation if their husbands are non-members or have no Christian commitment. Many are put off by the apparent complexity of the form-filling involved. Being gently talked through the issues can help enormously but is very time-consuming for the covenant secretary. However, it seems that those churches who achieve a high proportion of covenanted giving, either for special projects or mainstream support of their churches, have reached this point through taking the time to talk personally one to one with their members, perhaps by training up a special team of visitors. Those who leave the initiative with their members by just appealing for new covenanters through the weekly notices or in announcements from the front of the church fare much worse.

The Inland Revenue has issued guidelines to help charities produce their own covenant forms. These usually comprise two parts, the actual Deed of Covenant and the Bankers Order Form that instructs the donor's bank to carry out his/her wishes. The Deed of Covenant has to be witnessed by a third party, who like the donor needs to supply name address and signature, and who cannot be the donor's spouse. The date on the forms must precede the first actual payment from the bank. Covenants can only be taken out by UK taxpayers; the tax they have paid on the sum they have committed themselves to give can then be claimed back at intervals by the church or charity.

Some individuals are reluctant to engage in such a commitment because of uncertainty over their financial situation and needs so far into the future. However, the donor is able to withdraw from the commitment if his/her circumstances change, purely by instructing their bank to cancel the banker's order. It is helpful to the organization they have covenanted to if they also inform them of their change of plan.

Donations by covenant need careful monitoring. Banks are by no means infallible in putting their customers' instructions into force, and income from covenanters should be monitored to check that it is coming in as planned. Careful record-keeping is needed to identify what is net covenant income and what is straight cash income, and also to make sure that income claimed from the Inland Revenue tallies. Any discrepancies should be followed up, and deeds that have not been paid should be followed up with a courteous reminder letter. Covenants that run their course should be followed by a letter of thanks, an explanation of how the money has been used, and an invitation to take out a new covenant.

Gift Aid

Giving by Gift Aid was introduced by the government in 1990, and for the first time allowed individuals (and companies) to give a single sum of money to a charitable cause of their choice in a tax-efficient manner. The minimum gift eligible for this method was reduced in March 1993 to £250. The donor must be a UK resident when the gift is made, and must be a taxpayer to take advantage of the scheme. The gift must be in one lump sum rather than a series of smaller gifts. It cannot take the form of the writing off of a loan. It must be from one individual, though it can come from a joint account shared by that individual. N.B. Now that husbands and wives are treated separately for tax purposes, where one spouse has no independent taxable income it should be made clear that the donation is from the tax-paying spouse. He or she should keep the evidence that the donation was theirs alone, otherwise the Inland Revenue will deem that both shared the donation equally and only 50 per cent of the tax normally claimed by charities will be recoverable.

Gift Aid forms for individuals (R190 SD) and for companies (R240 SD) are available from the Inland Revenue, and it is advisable for any organization with charitable status to order a supply. When a gift that might be eligible is made the donor can be contacted and sent the relevant form to complete and return to the charity. The certificate is simple and easy to fill in, asking for name, address and confirmation of the amount given. The certificate must not be dated before the donation has actually been made. The donor's National Insurance number, Income Tax reference number and the address of his/her tax office is also requested. The church or charity then sends the forms off to the Inland Revenue to claim back the basic rate income tax paid by the donor. Some donors who give sums of £250 or above may not be aware of the scheme, and it is always worth mentioning the possibility and sending a form when you write to thank them and acknowledge their gift.

Deposited Covenants

This is becoming a rarer form of giving, and will probably become even more infrequent as giving through Gift Aid becomes more common. It is now only really relevant for single gifts under £250, as the Gift Aid procedure is far more straightforward for larger sums. Like ordinary covenants it can only be used by UK taxpayers, and must be witnessed by a person who is not the donor's spouse.

Basically it is a mechanism whereby a charity is able to gain immediate use of a total sum that a donor wishes to covenant. The organization is also able to claim back the tax immediately. It consists of two separate but interconnected transactions: an interest-free loan to the organization by the donor, repayable in four equal annual instalments, and a four-year covenant by the donor for an annual sum equal to one quarter of the loan. As the annual repayments of the loan by the charity exactly match the annual payments due from the donor under the covenant, they can be set off against each other, and no actual exchange of payments is necessary after the first cheque.

Again, charities can produce their own forms, using guidelines from the Inland Revenue. All forms should have two parts: the first being a Deposited Covenant form, covenanting a quarter of the total gift every year for four years to the chosen charitable cause. The second part is a combined letter of loan and waiver, using a recommended form of words, and witnessed by two individuals. This form, having been completed, should be sent with the cheque for the total net amount to be given to the church or charity, who than then include it in their next tax claim to the Inland Revenue. The dates on the cheque and the two parts of the form must all correspond. A copy of the form should be made by the recipient church or charity and sent to the donor to be filed with their official documents and will.

Gifts in kind

Some potential donors may find it difficult to give money, but may be able to help in more practical ways, by giving in kind. They may be able to give something that will be useful directly to the project you are raising money for – equipment for your building, furniture or fittings, or they may be able to give something that you can turn into money yourselves, with a little thought or imagination.

Local contacts may help you with the former. If you know that you have a need for office equipment, it may be that an office is closing down or relocating in your vicinity. Rather than gut the office and put perfectly serviceable equipment and carpet into a skip to be taken away and tipped, the owners may be willing for you to call by and take anything that you need. A friendly chartered surveyor may be able to tell you if guesthouses or small hotels are due to close or refit, releasing the possibility of secondhand kitchen and catering equipment.

Fundraising requests directly to small and medium-sized local businesses may well elicit more success attracting gifts in kind rather than cash. Small companies may be able to spare a sample of their product far more easily than cash. You then have the task of translating these gifts into hard currency. If you have no qualms about gambling, using them as raffle prizes is a simple way to do this; however, they can also be used in other ways, as items in auctions, as prizes for fundraising competitions or even, with the donor's permission, advertised for resale.

Legacies

In recent years the charity world and even Anglican dioceses have woken up to the great potential for income from legacies, the final supportive gesture a donor to your cause can make. Some may be uncomfortable with this concept, but it can actually be an extremely helpful thing to be able to gently direct adult members of your church and community to think of making suitable provision for those people and causes they care for when they die. Many people put this off until too late, and sadly would be horrified at the outcome of dying intestate. Several charities now issue leaflets on making wills, giving sound objective advice, alongside a gentle suggestion that their own charity be remembered alongside the other beneficiaries of the will. Certainly unless you are ashamed of the cause for which you are working, there seems to be no inherent reason why church people should not be encouraged to support local, national and para-church organizations in this way. For some charities legacy income remains one of their chief stand-bys, often bequeathed in general terms that allow them considerable freedom in the way that it is used.

A word of warning: any drive towards raising the profile of legacies within the church is likely to have a delay of at least four years before the first income results. Much of the fruit will come after years or decades have gone by. This is not a way of raising quick money for the immediate project you are now supporting! It is also true, as the costs of supporting a growing elderly population rise as we approach the new millennium, that there is likely to be less disposable income cascading down through the generations or entering the voluntary sector by this route. Too many houses and other capital savings are being expended in nursing home fees, eroding the amounts that used to be left in legacies.

Loans

Many campaigns run into a cashflow problem at some stage. Gifts will have been covenanted to the cause perhaps at an early stage of the proceedings, but the contractor's bills have to be paid long before the gross sum is received in full. Church authorities will often consider making quite substantial low-interest loans in such circumstances, and this will often enable a project to start sooner rather than later. It is also well worth canvassing for smaller loans from individuals, in addition to covenants and cash donations. Many will be willing to support a worthwhile cause in this way; while strenuous efforts should of course be made to be in a position to repay these at the end of the agreed term, it is a fact that many people will eventually be happy to turn their loan into a straight gift as the time for repayment draws closer, especially if there is still a shortfall to the overall total needed.

College example: Analysis of the Outdoor Activities Centre project income

The basic application devised for the St John's College Outdoor Activities Centre project is included as an example of an actual application at the end of Chapter 6. The actual results it elicited are described below.

In the early days of the campaign, a number of individual applications were sent to trusts who had the capacity to give a substantial proportion of the target sum for this project in one single grant, plus those who could give sums in the region of £2,000 to £5,000. This first tranche of applications resulted in the following donations:

£2,000 from a local trust which had supported aspects of the college's work in the past.

£2,000 from a trust based in the north of England with a declared interest in youth work; the correspondent paid a quick visit, unannounced, to see the site of the project before the decision was made.

£2,000 from a trust based in London with a declared interest in education and youth work (the arrival of the cheque was deferred until the money was needed to pay contractors).

£10,000 from a London-based trust with interests in social action and youth work, and with a strong Christian identity. We had initially applied to a larger associated trust with another project in mind, and had our application referred on. The amount was pledged, to be claimed when the money was needed to pay contractors. The trust secretary visited the college to tour the site after the pledge had been made but before it had been claimed.

A bank gave £2,500, a representative having attended the North-East launch of the campaign. We had to wait until the beginning of the next financial year for this to be approved, as the charitable budget for the current year had already been committed.

A businessman who attended the London launch of the campaign gave £2,500 from his company and a further £500 from his personal charitable trust.

A smaller Christian trust that had supported the college in the past gave £1,000. Another gave £100.

A local company gave £195.

After the two launches, all former students of the college received the basic campaign brochure describing our plans. A former student gave £2,500 by Gift Aid with the request that it be allocated to this project. Another supporter of the college who attended the North-East launch gave £400 by Gift Aid.

The sum raised was now sufficient to carry out major alterations to the ground floor of the building; it was decided to also attend to less substantial work required on the first floor at the same time, using money put aside in the main college budget for upkeep of buildings. This work was carried out over the summer vacation. The building itself was now ready to be used as a self-catering centre for visiting groups in vacations. Meanwhile through the academic year several students received training in canoeing skills and passed basic instructor's qualifications, using borrowed equipment.

A further amount now had to be raised to equip the centre, both inside the building and in terms of sports equipment. A concert by a visiting choir was held in Durham in July 1996 which raised £470. As a direct result, two canoes, spraydecks and paddles were later donated by individuals who attended the concert. A number of smaller trusts were identified and more applications sent out in the autumn, and further sums were received early the following year. Two trusts who had supported the college before gave £5,000 and £2,000 respectively and another trust new to us gave £3,000. Four smaller trusts gave further sums totalling around £1,000. Two hundred local businesses were also targeted; two gave donations of £50, and several more gave a surprising variety of gifts in kind valued at approaching £1,000, ranging from video tapes to gift vouchers, a painting by a local artist and a fridge-freezer. It was decided to hold a 'mystery auction' to convert these gifts into cash later in the year.

Having raised enough money to finish the conversion and equipping of the building itself, a small management committee was set up to administer the running of the centre. As attention was turned to financing the actual sports equipment, it was learned that another agency a few miles away which had been established by one of our former students was interested in sharing their equipment with us in a simple franchising arrangement. This provided an ideal way forward, generating some revenue income for them and reducing the capital amount we needed to raise before we could welcome the first groups in.

Points to remember

* Safeguard all cash donations and bank them as soon as possible.

* Train a team of visitors to help potential covenanters understand the process.

* Keep a supply of covenant, Deposited Covenant and Gift Aid forms readily available.

* Ask individual donors who give over £250 to consider Gift Aid.

* Be aware of useful gifts in kind that could be given, and plan ways to turn others into cash.

* Consider having a special legacy promotion programme – but don't expect quick results!

* Remember to include loans and pledges in the range of ways that supporters can help.

---

9 Administration

Basic office requirements

To set up any fundraising operation requires a basic minimum of physical resources, and attention should be given to these at an early stage. They include desk space, some office equipment, storage space for files, a telephone line, electricity and somewhere reasonably comfortable to work. As the campaign progresses, somewhere to meet potential donors also becomes a need.

Those churches or organizations which already possess an office may be able to integrate a small fundraising operation into their existing plant, especially if creative time-sharing of facilities is possible. Alternatively a spare room in the vicarage, an area of the vestry or within the home of a committed parishioner may provide a viable alternative. Sometimes a local business may be able to offer office space as a 'gift in kind', possibly being willing to carry postage, photocopying, electricity and/or telephone bills as an extra.

Minimum office equipment includes desk, two suitable chairs, telephone, filing cabinet, files, bookshelves, a typewriter and plenty of A4 paper. Adequate lighting is a must. There should always be room for at least two people to work together. Answerphones, faxes, PCs and printers make life much easier, as does access to a photocopier, and tea/coffee-making facilities and a heater will make unpromising situations bearable for the staff and volunteers. Internet access is a bonus! Some or all of these may be available on loan or as gifts from supporters.

Filing

A system should be devised to store all incoming and outgoing correspondence relating to the fundraising campaign. All prior correspondence and material relating to any other fundraising ever done by the organization should also be transported to the campaign administrative base, to be analysed and checked for potential contacts and to find out what has and has not worked in the past. At least two copies of each outgoing letter sent as part of the current campaign should be kept, using carbon paper if use of a PC is impractical. I have always found it helpful to keep a separate lever arch 'Day File' into which a copy of every item of correspondence is filed, with the other copy assigned to relevant named smaller files. If a PC is used there is also the capacity to keep outgoing correspondence on floppy disks which can be stored elsewhere and, if you have room, on your hard disk. Beware fire and theft, and regularly back up your material; a burglary or fire would be ten times worse if all your administrative material for your entire campaign disappeared too. It is good practice to keep your back-up disks in a completely different location for security.

Thank-yous
I don't believe it is possible to be too efficient in saying thank you. Anyone or any organization who has done you the immense favour of making a donation in today's financial climate when there are so many other calls upon their money deserves to be made a fuss of. I like to write to thank all donors within 24 hours if possible, with a letter that has a personal feel to it rather than a brief note of acknowledgment. Given the stresses and pressures of a fundraiser's life, this immediate response is not always possible but I aim for it whenever I can. Even when donors say that no response is necessary, I believe that the vast majority of people appreciate a genuine 'thank you' and will not grudge the expenditure on a stamp if it is necessary to post it – or the cost of a call to thank them in person.

It is also extremely good policy to keep your donors in touch with your progress. If you file your records carefully, it should be easy to keep track of your 'donorbase' or basic list of supporters. If you produce a newsletter from time to time, it is good to make sure that everyone who has shown interest or support gets one, with a covering letter which again feels as personal as possible. It can also be good to keep track of the dates on which donations arrive, and seek to write to people twelve months on from their first gift, to let them know of the progress you have made, and the way in which their donation has been spent. Such contacts can often elicit further donations virtually unsolicited, which more than pay for the postage involved, and which build up a sense of loyalty and commitment to your project.

Reports

Writing of regular reports can be time-consuming, but they serve an important purpose in the smooth running of any fundraising campaign. In the first instance, regular written reports allow your executive committee to be fully informed about your progress. Filed in tandem with the minutes of your committee meetings they will provide a definitive record of the course of your campaign. This in turn provides source material that will allow you to issue short bulletins on your progress, or articles for your newsletter. When you are immersed in a campaign that goes on for longer than a few months it can be difficult to remember the exact chronology of events or the actual dates when significant steps forward were taken. Checking your reports made at the time will mean that the facts will always be at your fingertips, and that the overall perspective of your achievements will be easy to convey. Recording your progress for posterity will also mean that your successors will have a sound basis to build on in the future.

Databases/card indexes

Accurate record-keeping is essential to the smooth running of a fundraising operation. This can be done by the use of card indexes, filed according to such categories as trusts, companies, individuals, churches, and each listing such information as full names, current addresses, date of last contact, gifts made, help offered, and the date of your next planned contact with that person or organization. More personal notes perhaps including subjective impressions or facts that might be useful to remember can be recorded on the reverse of the card. Alternatively, all this information can be kept on computer in the form of a database. A number of software packages are on the market designed specifically to help fundraisers keep useful fundraising databases, but most are priced out of the range of a small fundraising operation. It is quite possible for a basic software database package to be set up to meet your personal requirements adequately, with less expense. Whichever you opt for, it is important to keep records up to date, to ensure that spelling of names is correct and that the address listed is the current one. The system should be readily understood by all who have to use it.

Ledger books/spreadsheets

Detailed records of all income and expenditure relating to your fundraising should also be kept. If the fundraising operation is just a part of your organization's overall financial activity, it may be enough to keep exact receipts and payments records alone, leaving your treasurer to integrate these into the main income and expenditure picture, which will include such extra items as details of creditors, debtors, stock and depreciation, and distinguish any endowments or restricted funds.

You are likely to need a small petty cash fund to make day-to-day purchases for the running of the campaign. Never pay for these out of campaign cash income before it has been processed; instead draw a petty cash fund from the organization, and keep separate records in another ledger or spreadsheet, filing the receipts of all such purchases. After each purchase from petty cash, calculate your remaining balance and replenish the float when necessary from central campaign funds, making sure that these appear in your main campaign accounts. A third ledger book or spreadsheet may be necessary to track all covenanted and Gift Aided income, if you do not already have a covenants secretary overseeing this. Remember that the Inland Revenue expects charities and churches to ensure that people actually do give the amounts they have pledged in a covenant each year. Sometimes banks make errors implementing the Bankers Orders; sometimes individuals move, change bank, undergo a change of circumstances or die before the term of the covenant has expired; and these facts should be picked up before each claim for refunded tax is submitted.

Again there is a choice between 'hard copy' written in ledgers by hand, and computerized records stored in spreadsheet form, which can perform all sorts of breakdown and calculations at the touch of a few buttons. If you opt for the latter, it is imperative to keep regular printouts in a safe place so that a written record exists, and as with your written documents and databases, it is a wise precaution to back up the information on disk to protect you should disaster strike your computer. Transactions recorded in the accounts should be supplemented by further documentary evidence wherever possible. It is useful as a matter of routine when thanking donors to include mention of the date and amount received in the letter you write, even if you do not issue formal receipts. Income should be banked promptly both for the sake of the donor, and so that it is easier for you to trace incoming donations on your bank statements when reconciling your accounts. All expenditure should have copies of actual receipts to corroborate the amount paid. Where a team is involved in processing income and expenditure, the actual person dealing with it should initial and date the paperwork, so they can be identified if questions about it arise at a later date. Blank cheques should never be signed in advance and passed to another to perform the payment, to avoid any chance of cheque fraud. Many banks do not check signatures for cheques under a certain sum.

Setting a budget

Running a campaign office will inevitably involve cash expenditure, which should be seen as an investment in the ministry of your church or organization. It is sensible to set a realistic budget year by year to cover all the likely expenditure you will need to run the campaign. This will include most or all of the following: administrative salary costs, bills such as heating, light, telephone, rent, and expenditure on office equipment, postage, printing and photocopying, stationery, hospitality, travel, and any investment in merchandising or special occasions. It is also a good idea to build in a sum for miscellaneous items (often one-off items that do not sit easily in any of your other categories) and for contingencies, those unforeseen items which are bound to arise. Such provision can mean that you avoid going heavily into the red if disaster strikes, or that you have the leeway to invest in a sudden fundraising opportunity that may arise halfway through the financial year. The budget should be agreed upon in advance by your campaign committee and the organization as a whole, with special note being made of large sums needed at a particular time of year so that problems of cashflow are avoided. These basic running costs can legitimately be costed into the overall amount you are raising for your project, as long as you make it clear that you are doing this when approaching donors.

It is good to track your progress at key points through the year to make sure that you are not exceeding your budget targets, and to revise the sums involved up or down as appropriate. This detail will then help you set a realistic budget for the next year and so on. As with your other financial records, these can be kept on yet another spreadsheet, or in the form of hard copy in a ledger. Expenditure on administration should be clearly identifiable from expenditure on the actual project you are raising money for.

SORPS and the Charities Act

In 1996 the 1993 Charities Act came into force, bringing with it more stringent accounting regulations for all registered charities. The Charity Commission is now empowered to look into cases where charities do not comply. These regulations constitute recognized good practice, and although churches and small unregistered charities are exempt, it is nevertheless an extremely good idea for all treasurers to be familiar with them and to emulate them in keeping accounts. Guidelines for the production of annual reports and accounts (which now have to be made available to the public by law) are laid down in the form of a SORP (Statement of Recommended Practice), available with other leaflets on aspects of charity accounting from the Charity Commission. Certain kinds of charity such as housing associations have their own SORP, and if your charity happens also to be registered as a Company Limited by Guarantee, company law will take precedence over charity law. If you are not fundraising for a church, and are uncertain as to the law's requirements in your situation, you should contact the Charity Commission for advice as a matter of urgency.

Fraud

Sadly, the churches and Christian organizations are not immune to the risks of fraud, deception or theft, and there have been several high-profile examples both in Britain and elsewhere in recent years that have highlighted these dangers. Laxity of practice can lead to opportunity to yield to temptation by church members entrusted with care of the church's finances. Actual removal of cash is by no means the only problem. Falsification or alteration of accounting records and recording of unreal transactions so that theft remains unnoticed is also possible, along with misappropriation of other assets as well as money. The keeping of full accounts according to the SORP for a charity of comparable size, regularly scrutinized and with bank reconciliations regularly carried out, will help any irregularities come to light sooner rather than later. Problems, which may actually arise from ignorance rather than fraud, will thus be identified quickly rather than waiting until the year-end for detection.

Fraud in churches and charities usually either means the diversion of cash income into the individual's pocket before it reaches the stage where it is formally recorded, or the actual removal of funds, etc. already held which is subsequently covered up by alteration of records.

Fraud in churches and fundraising campaigns is much easier to accomplish than in commercial organizations. The income is totally unpredictable, and is not controlled by despatch notes, or invoices, or measurable against pre-set budgets. Who can predict what a jumble sale or concert will raise?

It is therefore to everyone's advantage that sensible steps are taken to minimize temptation and to share out elements of the processing of donations so that no one person shares the burden of suspicion if an item goes astray. The whole process should be looked at to eliminate opportunity for theft, bearing in mind the suggestions for appropriate administrative systems outlined earlier on in this chapter. The importance of observing any rules and checks brought into the system should be made clear for the benefit of all concerned.

College example: The development office

Prior to the setting-up of the development campaign, St John's College did not have a fundraising office as such, although a fundraising committee still met and some trust fundraising was still being carried out following on from a previous campaign in the 1980s. When the decision was taken to embark on a completely new campaign, I was appointed as fundraiser alongside my existing duties as pastoral tutor and alumni officer. I was given an office and a computer, and boxes of old files and correspondence from previous appeals. I was given a small budget to purchase directories, and to cover administrative costs. Given the total inexperience of the new fundraiser, the college wisely decided to invest in advice from a fundraising consultant for six months! The late Iain Mulholland was chosen, a man who well understood the worlds of higher education and the Church, and who had given similar sound advice in the earlier successful campaign of the 1980s.

From time to time volunteers have given valuable help in the office; for example when the main brochures first arrived, the principal's wife nobly spent many hours inserting full sets of information sheets into the back flaps – creating a rich supply that three years later is only just showing signs of running dry. Others have helped stuff envelopes for mailings at various times, and a recent graduate has created a 'web page' for me on the Internet. However, as the pace of work increased it became obvious that extra salaried help was needed, and three times now recent graduates have worked in the office for a year, giving invaluable help and in turn receiving some training in fundraising and office management. This has stood them in good stead as they have moved on to further careers in arts administration, the probation service and management consultancy. Although as the campaign approaches its final phase it has been decided that a full-time assistant is no longer justified, I now have a part-time assistant drawn from the tutorial staff, who covers the whole area of public relations for the college, and who specializes in applications to statutory sources of funding, relieving me of that particular burden.

The advent of increasingly sophisticated computer technology has meant that databases, spreadsheets and all written material can be easily produced and stored on computer. However, I have always made it my practice to keep hard copies of everything on file as well, just to be safe. All computer-stored material is backed up at intervals, with back-up copies stored away from the office in case of theft or fire. The filing system used by my predecessor was still intact and served as a perfectly adequate model for this campaign too. Churches, companies, trusts and statutory sources of funding all have their own drawers with files in alphabetical order, as do former students of the college, and other individual 'friends' and supporters. Another drawer holds details of training providers, sources of useful information, press cuttings, and the story of any special events organized along the way. Finally, there is a file for each individual project, recording its progress, and files servicing the various committees concerned with the fundraising process or with making the projects actually happen. Each letter and memo I write is also copied into large A4 lever arch 'day files', which reveal a chronological history of their own of the campaign as the years have gone by.

Finances are handled through the college's existing Finance Office. Donations come to me in the first instance; I record them on my own spreadsheet, and pass them to the Finance Office to be banked, writing immediate personal acknowledgments and thanks whenever possible. I also record pledges, keeping a running total of overall income, whereas the Finance Office deals strictly with actual money received, carrying out regular reconciliations with bank statements, and producing the definitive financial records for the auditors.

As the campaign reaches its final phase we are planning to scale down operations, taking the PR and alumni aspects of our work out of the mainstream work so that they can continue when fundraising diminishes, and reducing the total hours of salaried work undertaken.

My hope is that the records we keep will be of real assistance to fundraisers of the future, and that they will also have a place in the annals of the college when the next phase of its history comes to be written.

Points to remember

* Make sure the campaign workers have basic office equipment they need in order to function.

* Use an easily understood filing system.

* If you use computerized records and documents, back up regularly and keep hard copies.

* Update information such as changes of address regularly.

* Make and keep regular campaign progress reports.

* Process and acknowledge all donations promptly.

* Know the law and follow best practice in all financial procedures.

* Be aware of the risk of fraud.

PART TWO **DOING**

10 Direct giving

Many church communities tacitly assume that all aspects of their work and ministry should be funded by their members, using money tithed or given sacrificially directly to the Church. Some would go so far as to assert that adequate giving to support a particular development is one of the ways to judge whether it is within the will of God for it to go forward. Others may feel that while it is only right for church members to put their hands in their pockets for the regular ongoing expenses of maintaining church buildings, plant and staff, exceptional extra costs require exceptional means. The poorer the area and the people of the church, the harder it is to realistically see five- or six-figure sums being raised for substantial new projects. When a high proportion of members are living on benefits or pensions, a tithe of their disposable income may represent a great personal sacrifice, but amount to little in the face of the rising costs of mainstream church life.

Christian giving: the first priority!

However, if the decision is made that it is entirely appropriate to examine a variety of sources of external funding, perhaps including some or all of the areas outlined in this book, the local church should not regard itself as having been let off the hook. Many funders will examine carefully just how much effort has been put in at grassroots level to make a project happen before making their decision. They are likely to be impressed where any project has been given a substantial start by a local church or local supporters of a small charity through sheer sacrificial giving. It also gives a firm moral platform on which to stand when the church begins actively seeking further donations from others.

Some churches decide that in addition to raising money for their own project it would be good to raise a similar amount pound for pound to be given away, perhaps for a missionary organization or a project in the developing world. This can easily be put into practice in all giving from individuals, though it is difficult or impossible to carry this principle right through to donations from trusts, companies and statutory sources, all of which are likely to specify exactly what their contribution should be spent on.

Stewardship schemes

A wide range of stewardship schemes is now available. Many Anglican dioceses have adopted a particular approach, and have designated stewardship advisers on the staff. The schemes often focus on stewardship of time and talents as well as money, and provide a biblical framework to undergird their teaching. Following an established scheme can thus ensure that the congregation or basic nucleus of supporters understand the biblical basis for sacrificial giving, that common mistakes are avoided, and that answers are ready for the most common objections to asking individual church members to consider increasing their level of financial support. The demonstrable success of such established schemes in a variety of parishes or contexts can also be a powerful encourager and motivator for your own team.

Most stewardship schemes emphasize the need for training a group of lay people to be involved in the implementation of the scheme. One of the greatest predictors of the success of such schemes seems to be not just the inherent quality of the scheme itself, but the number of people of good standing in their church or organization who are willing to work through the background material carefully, and who subsequently volunteer to be trained to go out visiting their friends and neighbours to solicit support. This method can be particularly effective in getting occasional givers and those on the fringes of church life to become regularly committed, and to consider making their regular gift in the form of a covenanted donation. The process of making a covenant is still a mysterious, slightly threatening thing to many, who may be put off by the form-filling, the legally binding nature of what they are doing, and the worry of taking on a regular commitment for four years in today's uncertain world, and who may have a weak grasp of the benefits to the cause they support. To have a trusted and reliable friend available to talk them through the issues involved and to reassure them about the procedure and the nature of the commitment may make all the difference – particularly if that person can speak to them with all the moral authority of one who has themself decided to give by this method.

Gift days

Many churches already organize gift days, or days on which pledges can be made for the coming year, allowing the church to budget properly for the future. Sometimes these are an emergency measure, with the funds needed immediately to meet crises in funding in the church. Often, however, there is a conscious aspiration that regular giving should be enough to deal with regular items in the church's year, leaving gift day income for special projects or to give away.

Timing of such gift days can enhance their effectiveness, as can the teaching from the pulpit or in other groups, which prepares the way before them. Pentecost, Harvest and Christmas all lend themselves to themes of thankfulness and giving, as does the patronal festival or anniversary of the church's foundation. Sometimes the gift day can be the first overt fundraising activity taking place to support a project or scheme. Much can depend on the results; it is possible for a substantial proportion of the total needed to come in in just 24 hours, especially if personal pledges of giving (covenanted if appropriate) are sought as well as cash.

Approaching local people

Most church people would agree that only those who are committed church members should be approached to take on planned giving to support the regular work of the church. However, where a project is likely to have a positive impact on the life of the community, and has been designed to serve the needs of local people, an argument can be made that a much wider group can be approached for financial support. If sensitively done, this can actually provide an opportunity to let local people know what you are doing and that you are interested in serving them. It may be that some new potential members of the church or clients for the service you are offering are first contacted through a visiting programme that explains your plans.

Public charitable collections

This is the phrase used in the Charities Act to cover charitable appeals made in a public place or by means of visits from house to house. The legislation specifically excludes such appeals made in the course of public meetings or on land occupied for the purpose of a place of public worship. Collections at services are therefore exempt!

All collections undertaken in public places need special permission, either through application for a permit from the local authority or authorized by order of the Charity Commissioners. Contravention of this is an offence punishable by a fine. The local authority can set certain conditions when issuing a permit, by specifying the day of the week, date, time or frequency of the collection. They can refuse permission, where for example they believe that undue inconvenience to the public might be caused, or where there would be a clash with another collection. There is a right of appeal if permission is refused.

Those collecting on behalf of the charity will need proper identification – badges and certificates of authority – to inform the public that they are authorized to take part in a properly organized and legal charitable collection. Those holding collecting cans or jars in public places should be informed that it is now an offence to draw attention to their cause by rattling or shaking the container. It is good practice for all containers to be sealed at the end of the collecting session, taken to a safe place and the contents counted and recorded as soon as possible, in the presence of witnesses, before being stored securely and banked at the earliest opportunity.

Door-to-door visiting

It may be appropriate for a team of visitors to be set up in the church to go door-knocking, with special training to prepare them for the likely reactions they may receive. This team may visit areas of your parish or catchment area systematically to canvass support. A map of the parish, or the local electoral register lists, could be used to divide up the area into manageable chunks for small teams. It is possible to offer a variety of ways in which people might help, some of which would not involve straight cash gifts, and would therefore be possible for anyone, however low their income. Options could include being willing to fill in a brief questionnaire about their views of the project, voluntary help, being involved in a future fundraising event, or prayer. Those visited could also be asked whether they feel the church could be doing more for them, and whether they have any pastoral needs, or a desire to know more about the Christian faith. Careful debriefing after such visiting is needed to make sure that all those who have responded positively or who wish for closer contact with the church are followed up by the clergy or pastoral visitors.

Segmentation

When considering approaching the public directly for money, many charities will consider breaking down the geographical area they are targeting into different groups or segments and approaching each in a slightly different way according to what is known about the population's lifestyle, opinions or capacity to give. It may be that with a little extra thought and preparation, this approach could help a local church or organization raise a larger amount of funding than a blanket appeal to everyone.

Type of housing is one obvious way that local knowledge can give an indication of varied capacity to give. It may be worth individually prepared approaches to large detached houses where the wealthier inhabitants are likely to live, having first researched whether any of their family members have used the church for weddings, baptisms or other occasions in recent years, or whether they have any known links to local charities or other discernible reasons for supporting you. Money may not be the only or the main thing to ask for in the first instance; they might be willing to offer their garden for an event or to help in other practical ways. At the other end of the scale, there may be other areas that the church feels uncomfortable about approaching for money because of the extent of deprivation there. Using sensitivity and knowledge of local people and local issues will help you come to a sensible decision. Discuss your plans with members or supporters who actually live in the different areas to get a sense of whether you are getting the balance right.

In your written material, it can be effective to highlight different issues to different 'markets' within the area you are targeting for help with your campaign. For example, covering letters can contain one particular paragraph that relates your activities to the particular concerns held by members of that group. The more middle-class constituency may still value the existence of the church building and the traditions of the Church and be willing to contribute to a fund for the heating system or the church bells, even if their appearance at church is limited to major festivals; in areas with high youth unemployment or a drug problem, drop-in centres for young people may meet a need that is universally recognized, and in an area where crime is high and elderly people live in fear of muggings, lunch clubs and pastoral visiting schemes can show that the church is doing something positive to meet the needs of the community and deserves support from the wider public. Think which of your range of activities are particularly relevant to the people you are approaching, and make sure that they know about the good things you are already doing.

Community groups

Many churches and church-owned properties are used by a variety of community groups. Some church members may have key leadership roles in others. It may be possible to approach these groups to engage in a fundraising activity or event on your behalf. This may lead to a closer liaison and relationship between the group and the church in the future. The church could mark its appreciation of such support by inviting its representatives to any special thanksgiving or festivities when the project is opened. Local schools may be willing to embrace the project in a similar way, opening a door to closer contact with the children of your neighbourhood.

College example: The Multi-Media Studio

Two years into the campaign the Centre for Christian Communication (CCC) was ready to begin functioning. Premises had been earmarked within the former hospital wardblock purchased by the college and renovated that summer (a distinct campaign project). Funding for the director's post had been secured in full for the first twelve months through a partnership of two major charitable trusts, with a diminishing commitment for four further years. On 1 September that year the first director took up his post.

Very soon a further need became pressing – for equipment to allow the director to begin his active role. The equipping of a multi-media studio to serve the centre and to provide training facilities for local community groups and small businesses had been seen as the final piece of this particular jigsaw. The time had come to locate that piece to complete the picture. In the very short term, initial activities could be served by ferrying individual items of equipment up from the main college site (as long as they weren't needed simultaneously in two places at once), or by hiring in specific items for specific occasions. Obviously, this situation was far from ideal and could not be allowed to go on indefinitely.

Most usual sources of funding for the centre had already been tried for other projects in the development campaign; namely trusts, companies and individuals. Alumni had already been approached for gifts for refurbishment of college buildings and for the student Hardship Fund, as it was felt that funds for these two projects would be unlikely to be found outside the college 'family'. The centre was not eligible for statutory funding because of its distinctive Christian basis. It was therefore decided to explore the possibility of a direct-mail operation to churches in the north of England, seeking one-off gifts to provide an influx of capital to provide basic equipment.

It was also important to find out the likely take-up of the centre's services from local churches, and it was decided to combine a direct-mail fundraising exercise with a simple market research operation. A covering letter described the potential role of the centre and its current urgent need for equipment. It asked the help of churches in the Diocese of Durham and two Anglican dioceses bordering Durham (Newcastle and York), setting out a number of ways in which this could be usefully forthcoming, including a donation at some point over the coming financial year, sharing insights into other possible sources of funding, filling in a questionnaire enclosed in the mailing, going onto a mailing list to receive further details as the centre developed, and prayer support. It was decided that if this exercise proved successful, it would be extended to other denominations, and to other northern dioceses, as the centre was established to serve the whole northern region.

In addition to the covering letter and the questionnaire, a sheet of precise equipment costs was included, listing items priced from £50 to £3,000 each. The relevant information sheet produced for the campaign brochure was also included to illustrate the original vision of the centre in full. Finally, the centre's first marketing leaflet giving a flavour of things to come was added, plus a freepost envelope addressed to the college, allowing responses to be made quickly and easily without needing a stamp.

Points to remember

* Biblical teaching on giving will prepare the way for individual Christians to make their response.

* Consult a few stewardship schemes before making your choice.

* Regular or occasional gift days can be part of the 'mix'.

* Consider if it is appropriate to seek funds from local people.

* Remember that door-to-door visiting and street collections are governed by special regulations.

* Consider segmenting your approach according to different social factors.

* Do ask community groups who use your facilities for support.

---

11 Big gifts

Why bother?

A typical fundraising campaign needs to raise a relatively small number of substantial gifts to fulfil its true potential. Each single such gift made has the power to advance the amount you have raised by a significant percentage towards your target. A sizeable gift before you announce to the world at large that you are fundraising at all is the best possible start. Every fundraiser has limited resources of time and energy, particularly if the organization they work for is itself small, and other tasks demand their attention alongside the raising of money. It therefore makes sense to prioritize, and to place the seeking of substantial individual donations high up that list of priorities.

Research

The key to raising large amounts of money from single sources lies in research. You have to identify sources with the capacity to give big sums. Within those sources (primarily rich individuals and the larger trusts) you must work hard to identify which ones might possibly have a reason to give to you. Just knowing that key individuals have a strong Christian commitment is a help but is not enough on its own. Try to build up a dossier on the key individuals you have identified, from *Who's Who* and similar publications, from the press and from snippets of information that your advisory group can tell you. Circulate lists of targeted trustees, directors and philanthropic individuals to them, asking if they know them or know of any reason why they might support your cause. Go back through the parish records – have any members of their families had contact with the church, maybe through occasional services? Did any of them go to school with any of your contacts?... belong to any of the same clubs?... mix in the same social circles? If your contacts are convinced of the value of your project they may be willing to bring it to the attention of their friends or acquaintances.

Emphasize to all your supporters that no one is to make contact with a potential donor without your knowledge. Social networks being what they are, especially in the regions, it is not uncommon for several of your advisory group to know the same person. You have to sort out which of them would be best placed to commend your cause. Nothing can take the wind out of your sails more effectively than to set up a meeting, then find that Joe Bloggs has already told them all about you, possibly without the finely tuned emphasis that you know would be most likely to elicit support. At worst this can look like gross inefficiency and deter your target from thinking seriously of supporting you.

Motivation

People give for a variety of reasons. Sometimes the motive is purely altruistic. Sometimes there is a desire for a memorial to a loved one. Sometimes there is a desire to make a personal gesture that will make them feel good, or which will enhance their standing in the community. Sometimes there is guilt. Sometimes there is a subtle mixture of several of these at once. Gaining a sense of what makes a person tick can help you decide how exactly to make the all-important approach to them. The stage of a person's career can also be significant. A newly retired captain of industry, with energy, skill and range of contacts intact but looking for a new direction in life, can be open to more of a commitment than a thrusting young executive with horrendous work pressures, long hours, a huge mortgage and a family to support.

Peer group pressure

Those involved in fundraising for good causes have learned that there are ways and means of asking for money. Some can be spectacularly more effective than others. One of the least likely to succeed is to write a letter with no prior personal contact and just ask. In contrast, it seems that one of the most effective methods is to bring an aspect of peer group pressure to bear. Wherever possible it is good to get someone personally known to your target to ask on your behalf. That person should be well briefed and be able to speak knowledgeably about your plans. Unless they feel strongly that it would be counterproductive it can be helpful for them to arrange a three-way meeting, with a representative of the campaign present also. The intermediary should be a genuine supporter of yours, and most importantly should have already made a donation themself to your funds. They are then in the strongest possible moral position to ask their friend to give also, being totally open and up-front about it, without a hint of apology.

A middle way, if your contacts feel that they do not know your selected potential donor well enough to ask directly on your behalf, is to get them to ring informally to ask whether the targeted person would be willing to offer an appointment for you to visit them. Your contacts may feel more comfortable asking half an hour of their time than for money. The ball is then in your court to follow this opportunity up, making of it what you can. Another option, if your contact has a more tenuous link with the target, is to write a letter yourself to the target person, mentioning your mutual acquaintance with your contact, and saying that your contact had suggested the letter, thinking that the target person might be interested in your campaign.

Gifts with strings

Big-gift fundraising is all about relationships with individuals. Because they are individuals they may wish to give in unusual ways or lay down conditions linked to their donation. These must be taken seriously and their implications thought through. Do you really want to accept a valuable work of art as a gift in kind if you do not have the facilities to look after it securely, and there is a proviso that it should never be sold? Is a large brass plaque commemorating the donor on the front door of your building appropriate? Is the whole organization happy that the project becomes the Harry Smith Church Hall or the Jane Jones Youth Scheme? It may be that they are, but the implications should be thought through and any wider issues tactfully addressed before you bank the money. Some donors may consciously or unconsciously expect from now on that they have the right to approach the organization at any time in the future for return favours, and to expect individual attention from those who were involved in the negotiations concerning the gift. This may lead to embarrassing situations in the future, for example where they conflict with established church practice. Do everything you can to make clear that by accepting a substantial donation you are not in any way selling influence over the running of your church or organization.

Donor care

Once your target person has given to you, that should by no means be the end of the story. Thanking and acknowledgement of the gift should be prompt and efficient. Information bulletins about your progress should follow. If the gift has taken place before your public launch (if you are having one) the donor should be invited, and in any case they should be invited to the opening or a celebratory event for the project when the target has been raised and the work done. Sometimes donors wish to give their money without fuss and make it clear that this was a one-off donation, discouraging further contact. Others will give because they identify with you, and will continue to follow your progress. Some donors may become so committed that in time they give to you again and even again and again. It is never good to seek for further money too soon, but in some cases it is possible to build on the relationship to the extent that the donor will be willing to offer you time and further advice. He or she may bring a further network of contacts who may be sympathetic, and introduce you to other sources of funding. In the best possible scenario, they might even be drawn into your advisory group.

Relationships are at the heart of our faith. Whoever the donor is, as soon as a donation has been made, that person enters a new phase of relationship with you. It is then up to the church to foster that relationship, not just with the narrow motive of financial gain, but with the open and honourable intention to share more of the life of God's people with those who have chosen to use their time and efforts on your behalf. Most people do not have a sudden conversion through a blinding flash of revelation. Most grow into faith, often through a process of being drawn gradually closer in to the heart of a Christian community. It just may be that contact through fundraising activity is a small link in the chain. It can be easy to forget this in the heat of a major fundraising push!

College example: The unexpected donor; the Urban Mission Centre

Two examples for this chapter, but one of them is very short!

Carrying out several jobs in addition to fundraising for the college means that I get a lot of mail, some of it through the normal post, and some of it through the university's 'internal mail' which runs between the other colleges, departments and central university administration. It's therefore not unusual to receive quite a few anonymous-looking envelopes, sometimes heavily recycled, in the course of the day. It just so happened that on a certain occasion I missed one which had been pushed under the door, then placed on a pile of other papers, not opening it until it had lain there for some time.

I have heard experienced fundraisers sometimes say that each campaign has at least one unexpected piece of luck (or blessing, depending on your theological perspective) which will come its way. That anonymous brown envelope certainly contained ours. It contained a cheque for £40,000 together with an admonition that the donation be kept absolutely anonymous. I had to look at it several times before the amount sank in, and the number of noughts made sense. The donors were friends of the college, who knew the institution well and who obviously felt that what we were doing was worth supporting to a substantial extent. Having no idea that they had the capacity to make such a gift, they had not received the full charm offensive from us! It was good to know that people who knew us well, warts and all, still felt it right to give so generously. The gift was directed towards the Christian ministry of the college. Apart from the then college accountant who actually banked the cheque, I have been able to maintain the anonymity of the donors completely. No other staff know their identity.

The second example also reflects the importance of personal contact in the chain of progression that leads to a donation.

Some years ago, a highly placed executive in a medium-sized British company sensed a call into ordained Anglican ministry, and gave up his job to train at Cranmer Hall. Although by the time the development campaign came into being he was ordained and serving his title in a parish miles from Durham, he maintained his links both with his former colleagues and with the college. He suggested that two of these colleagues be invited to the public launch of the campaign at Lambeth Palace, and wrote personally to encourage them to attend, which they duly did. Without the obvious respect and esteem which this young clergyman's former colleagues obviously still held for him, I doubt if they would have bothered to accept our invitation; the quality of the relationship they had with him was a very strong link in this particular chain.

The company had a policy of giving to causes that made a real difference to deprived communities. Their attention was caught by aspects of the 'community' strand of our campaign, particularly our plans to develop an outdoor activities centre for youngsters in one of our college buildings, and to fund a youth and community worker in a run-down area of Gateshead to work with the team vicar there in a community centre next to his church. This vicar had a dual role as director of the college's Urban Mission Centre, where ordinands went to spend time gaining insight into the particular needs of inner city areas, and learning strategies to tackle the immense needs ahead of them if their own future ministries lay in such areas.

The two representatives of the company who attended the launch felt that it was worth sending a third executive to Durham, to see if our projects might fit the type of cause they liked to support. She spent several hours with us, taking time to get a real grass-roots feel for the college and what we were about. The outcome? Some weeks later we heard that the company was prepared to fund the post of Youth and Community Worker in full for three years. This was a tremendous boost to us at the time; the first project to move entirely from vision to reality, and one that would have such a positive impact on a local community that suffered all sorts of disadvantages. Subsequently an experienced community worker was appointed to the post, taking up her appointment some months later.

Points to remember

* Each substantial gift advances your cause significantly.

* Do as much research as you can first.

* Analyse a potential donor's motivation.

* Remember the power of peer group pressure.

* Think hard about any strings attached before accepting.

* Look after your donors!

---

12 Charitable trusts and foundations

What's special about trusts?

Fundraising from charitable trusts is a particular specialty within fundraising as a whole. Unlike most other sources of funding, trusts actually exist to give their money away. Cumulatively they give over £500 million to charities and the voluntary sector in the UK each year. They fund an enormous range of activities, sometimes consciously seeking out unpopular causes. Information about many trusts is publicly available, with contact names and addresses published in directories that make it easier for you to single them out and make your application.

However, these bonuses are countered by certain disadvantages. For example, trusts can only give according to their charitable objects. If your cause is ineligible there is nothing that can be done about it. The sums available are finite, and all trusts receive far too many applications for the funds they have at their disposal. They operate according to their own timescale of agendas and meetings; only in exceptional circumstances can they hurry things up to fit in with your preferred timing, however urgent your need. Many trusts already know who they want to give their money to and will not consider speculative applications. Even for those who invite open applications, increasing use of word processors means the number of reasonably presented requests they receive is rising all the time. As described in earlier chapters, it is comparatively easy now for fundraisers to send off a high number of applications with only minor modifications.

Selecting your shortlist

As in all spheres of fundraising, meticulous research comes first. From all the sources open to you, a trust list of manageable proportions should be drawn up. This can be taken primarily from directories, but if you have records of any past donations from trusts or any good links with them, make that trust a priority for another application. Many trusts keep a low profile and do not wish to appear in trust directories for fear of being deluged with applications; however, further information may be available directly from the Charity Commissioners, where all trusts now have to be registered, or from local authorities and from local charities information services. Personal contacts may unearth other possibilities. Networking with other fundraisers can be invaluable.

Go through the directories and look closely at the objectives of each trust. Where possible glean information on the kind of projects they are actually funding to help you select which aspect of your project to emphasize in your application. Some projects may benefit a range of people, and it can be useful e.g. to highlight specific benefits to the elderly or to young where appropriate. However, remember that if you ask for funding for a specific aspect of your work, and a trust agrees to donate to that area, you must be able to demonstrate at the end of the day that the money was spent on the purposes for which it was given and did not end up in the general 'pot'.

Making contacts

If you have been able to identify any personal links between your network of supporters and trustees of various trusts, now is the time to bring these into play. The trusts appearing on your list can be further graded according to the warmth of contact you have with them. The warmer your contact, the greater your chance of success in interesting them in your plans, and ensuring that you receive due attention and a reasonable hearing. This grading process will help you to judge the trusts most likely to respond to your application. Your system might go something like this:

Boiling! If someone in your church or organization knows a trustee well enough to be able to speak to them personally about your project, get them to ask for an appointment for you both to meet to talk about it, or offer an invitation for them to visit. The emphasis at this stage is to ask purely for a little of their time. Once they have met you in person a trustee is much more likely to share your enthusiasm if the project really is a good one, and become an advocate for you during the formal trustees' meeting to discuss the next tranche of grants. They can talk to you about the issues that may crop up in discussion among other trustees, and may be able to offer guidance about the kind of information they will want to know.

Hot The next best option is to use any contact of genuine stature, perhaps a respected local expert or member of the church hierarchy, to make the same kind of contact. The higher up the social or ecclesiastical scale your contact may be, or the higher the public perception of their expertise in the field you are active in, the harder it can be for your targeted trustee to ignore their views. Again, remember that you are seeking an opportunity to commend the project and win a friend who can speak for you. You are not trying to distort or bypass the application procedure or gain an unfair advantage over applications from other sources. You are trying to ensure that by the time your application is formally considered by the trustees of that particular trust, at least one person present can speak knowledgeably about you, sharing their honest perception of the value of what you are trying to achieve, and your suitability to achieve it.

Warm If your time is limited, it might be worth arranging a visit for representatives from a range of trusts who fund your kind of project to meet you *in situ* to see the context of your application and to meet selected supporters and potential beneficiaries. They can also visit the site of your project and attend a specially prepared presentation. Although such functions take time and money to arrange, if done properly, they should pay for themselves many times over in future donation income. Remember that your campaign launch provides a unique opportunity to impress. Many of the larger trusts are aware of each other's work, and some local trusts may meet informally from time to time to discuss their policies. Support from one trust may thus lead to awareness of the value of your work among others in the network. You may find that another trust takes you seriously because they know that X or Y Trusts only give to worthwhile and sound projects.

Tepid Where there is no warm contact, the next best approach could be for the fundraiser to take the initiative and ask for a visit or contact either from any trustees who happen to live locally, or from the administrator, secretary or correspondent of the trust. This can be a mutually helpful fact-finding exchange, designed to save both of you time and energy at a later stage by making sure that your application is framed appropriately.

Cool Where a telephone number is given in trust directories, unless contact by phone is specifically discouraged it can be assumed that a quick call to ascertain that your application is on the right lines and has a realistic hope of receiving consideration can be helpful. Again, it helps both parties know that they are not wasting their time, and helps your eventual application have a better chance of success. Your call can be followed by a carefully targeted written approach.

Freezing Unsupported haphazard written applications fired off to trusts in general are sure to fail miserably, wasting your time and money and frustrating the recipients at the trust's end.

Treat each trust as special

Even if your contacts are not willing to go out on a limb for you and to use the contact you feel would help you so much, you may find their knowledge of the trust scene extremely helpful. Trusts are idiosyncratic entities, and can have very different characteristics. Some will have enthusiasms for particular types of project and dislike for others. They may reflect the foibles and characteristics of their founders, or those in whose memory they were established. They may have very differing ways of assessing the applications that come their way, and their secretaries or correspondents may have particular enthusiasms or dislikes concerning the way applications are laid out. The more you know the wiser you can be. Keep in mind that you are writing to an individual at the same time as to an organization. That individual may have to open hundreds of applications a week. He or she will have a fine-tuned instinct, able to detect whether you have done your research adequately and whether you have put time and effort into your application. They may also be able to tell if you have included their trust as part of a mass mailing. It is frighteningly easy to insert the name of the wrong trust or correspondent if you are producing a large number of applications at once. I have done it myself. Even if you get that right, trusts are so different that one covering letter and one stock application is unlikely to be ideal for them all. It is worth taking the time to personalize each one, consulting the directories to customize your basic text to their requirements and interests. For example, you may be able to quote support they may have given in the past for similar projects as a reason for your application, to show that you have thought things through before choosing them as a potential source of funding.

Timing

The timing of your application is extremely important when seeking funds from charitable trusts. Many meet only annually, every six months or quarterly. A brief telephone call can establish when the deadline is for applications for the next meeting of trustees. If the trustees are not meeting for another ten months, that particular application can go on the back burner for a while. It can also be useful to check out how quickly you are likely to hear the verdict. Some trusts send out a brief card acknowledging your application, and saying that if you hear nothing within a specified time you must assume that your application has been unsuccessful. Others may send individual letters. Some ask for a stamped addressed envelope to cut down their own administrative costs. Often the reason for a negative response is pure over-subscription of available funds rather than anything intrinsically wrong with your application. However, when you have had a good conversation in the past with one of the trust's personnel, you may feel able to call again and talk about the decision, to see if there are any lessons you could learn, and to check if a future application with a different emphasis might be possible after a while.

If they say 'no'...

Statistically speaking, a refusal from a trust is the most likely response that you will receive, but it need not be the end of the story. Unless they specifically discourage contact, in which case you will only annoy them by seeking further advice, you may be able to maintain a relationship with them. The letter you receive may give some hint as to the reason; if not and the trust publishes a telephone number, use it to make a quick call to try to establish the reasons. If their decision appears to be based on a fallacy or misunderstanding, let them know. If they feel that you are seeking an amount that is too high, try to identify something else within the project that falls within their scale of giving and apply again for that instead. If they say that all their giving is currently committed to another project, contact them again in a few months time, to find out if funds will become free again in a year or two, and if the answer is yes, bear that in mind for future applications. Whatever the reason, unless specifically advised not to, consider applying to each trust again, possibly for something different, in a year's time. Gentle persistence can pay dividends.

College example: The college entrance hall

Alongside the more innovative projects within the development campaign which emphasized aspects of the college's work, lay the need to maintain the college buildings. These mainly began life as a series of

Georgian houses on the Bailey, the old cobbled street running past the cathedral and castle on the peninsular which forms the ancient heart of the city of Durham. They provide a much-loved but often crumbling rabbit warren of corridors and passages, flights of stairs and unexpected corners and dead ends, held in great affection by generations of students. The demands of English Heritage on the one hand (many of the buildings are listed) and the fire safety officers on the other have had deep and sometimes expensive implications for the college for many years.

The main college entrance lies in No 3 South Bailey. The heavy wooden doors, temptingly ajar, formed a key symbol for the campaign, appearing on the front cover of the brochure. Within the doors lay a small hallway, flanked by a wall to an outer and inner office to the left, and the broad sweep of a fine but neglected staircase up to the right. Half obscured by the outer office wall and doorway, the evidence of half an archway pointed to a rather grander layout in the past. The college decided to give priority to this entrance area, in order to impart a 'sense of arrival' for all visiting the college, to create a spacious and comfortable reception area and office, and to restore the staircase to something much closer to its former glory.

A trust which had supported the college in the past when working on another college building in the 1980s was selected as being one of the most likely to lend support to this project. One of our advisory group knew a current trustee personally. At an early stage in the campaign I had had the opportunity to meet the trust's secretary, who had been charm personified in his kind welcome to a novice fundraiser on her very first trip to London in her official capacity! This trust was one of the few we could find which was prepared to give useful sums of money for work on buildings, although there was obviously a need to prove significant architectural merit.

We began to research and create our basic case for support. Local guidebooks were perused and quotes extracted concerning the merit of the house and staircase. The story of the original inhabitant, Sir Robert Eden (who had the house built and who moved there in 1739 with his young bride, living there happily and producing 11 children before his untimely death at the age of 38), was written up, and Sir Robert's latest descendant contacted and canvassed for further details. Plans were drawn up, photographs taken to illustrate the current less-than-ideal situation, and the whole project was related to the growth of the college in recent years and put into the context of the wider campaign. Other work recently carried out on the building by the college was also listed with costs, so that the college was shown to be making efforts to help itself.

Several letters were sent back and forth between the college and the trust before the application came to receive formal consideration by the trustees. The college had to make a strong case to show that the work involved was actually restoration (which was supported by the trust) and not mere refurbishment (which lay outside their guidelines). Aspects that could be seen as just refurbishment were removed from the application (such as internal doors, decoration, wall and floor finishes). The college architect was pressed to provide further details of the actual work involved on more than one occasion.

The end result, nearly nine months after the first tentative contact with the trust, was a grant large enough to cover a significant proportion of the necessary work. Because the grant was not made until late July, it was not possible for contractors to be engaged to do the work that summer, and it was eventually completed early the next year. The college entrance hall has provided a pleasant and practical area to welcome all comers, in perfect keeping with such a gracious building, ever since.

Points to remember

* Trusts exist to give money away!

* Draw up a realistic list of target trusts whose criteria match your needs closely.

* Utilize all possible contacts for extra insight, and an introduction of some kind.

* Grade your targets and focus your efforts.

* Check the timing.

* Personalize your application as much as possible.

* If they say 'no' this time, try to leave a door open to re-apply in future.

---

13 Companies

Directories

In many ways the starting-point in looking at companies as a source of charitable giving is very similar to that of charitable trusts. There are directories of company giving which may give useful details of companies which support your kind of project. These may be ordered by your library if you do not have spare money to invest in your own copies. They will also list names of chief executives, managing directors, other members of the board of directors, and those within the company who have responsibility for overseeing the charitable budget. In addition, many companies publish glossy annual reports, which you can request and which may give further hints about their preferred areas of giving.

However, even more than in the case of trusts, it is important to get all your information clear and up to date before you start. A simple telephone call will usually elicit the right person for you to address your letter to. Job mobility is such these days that many names mentioned will be out of date by the time the directory reaches your shelves. It does not look good if you address your initial application for money to a chief executive who retired under a cloud, accompanied by heavy media coverage, twelve months before!

As with trusts, a personal link may get you a hearing. If a company is local, or has a local subsidiary, and especially if your parishioners or the users of your project are either a target market of, or employees of, the company concerned, you have a far higher chance of a successful application. It is worth undertaking widespread research into lists of directors of your target companies to find out if any of your contacts know them personally, and could arrange an appointment for you to see them.

Unlike trusts, companies are in business to make money for their shareholders, and emphatically do not exist to give their money away.

There is no point in making applications to them if you do not fit the criteria for their giving programmes exactly. Many will have an additional agenda, which may or may not be explicitly acknowledged, of wanting something back from you, looking to their association with you to enhance their image or their market in some way. It is worth thinking through what you might have to offer them and committing this to writing at some point in your application.

Local companies

These days the trend is against large companies making indiscriminate donations to a wide range of charities. Many now have highly sophisticated programmes to support various charities, and look for some sort of substantial pay-back in return, whether it be in terms of good publicity and PR, or a higher level of satisfaction among their employees. Even if the boom years for the economy in Britain return, companies are likely to remain highly selective in their giving.

Small local projects may therefore find it far more fruitful to look at small or medium-sized local businesses for support. The local chamber of commerce may produce directories of local businesses. So may your local authority's Economic Development Unit. Your members and supporters may even work in some of them. Thomson directories, Yellow Pages telephone directories, and even a drive round your local industrial estate may reveal more potential donors. At the very least, you should be able to build up a list of local suppliers used by your church or organization, who may value you custom, and who therefore may be willing to offer some support.

The business pages of your local paper will cover stories about regional activities of national companies as well as the local companies. These will sometimes be accompanied by photographs of managing directors or chief executives, which you could build up into a local file of information. Some companies will give away a percentage of their turnover or profits, and it can be helpful to know which companies are doing well and are likely to have a surplus at any time.

Use your contacts!

Once again, the establishing of personal contacts is important. Do any of your members or volunteers, or their spouses or relatives, work for a significant local employer? Do they know if a good cause is being adopted for the year as part of company giving? Would they be willing to pass on a request for support for your project to the relevant person in the company? Can they feed back to you what that company might appreciate in return; perhaps a photo opportunity in the local press, or an invitation to a special event where they might meet other potential business contacts socially? Would the gift of some time by employees of the company be useful to the project, perhaps as volunteers, or for a particular fundraising activity, perhaps sponsored in aid of the project? Companies tend to be far more favourably inclined to give support to causes where there is involvement and a groundswell of support among their staff.

Who is looking for a profile?

Sometimes companies are keen to raise their profile or change their image in a particular area. Being aware of this can help you time your application for maximum receptivity on the part of the company. Perhaps the company has had a bad press recently (be careful, this may have been for justifiable reasons, and you may want to think through if you actually want to be associated with them). Perhaps they are engaged in a particular battle for sales in your area (but do you want to be seen as taking sides?). Perhaps they are launching a new product or promotion. Perhaps they are expanding (adverts for jobs in the local press may be one indication of this). Perhaps they have just opened up in your area and wish to create a positive image for themselves locally in as short a time as possible.

Sponsorship

It is rare to find companies who will give for purely altruistic motives. Most will look for something in return. This means that in the eyes of the law a high proportion of support for charitable causes from the corporate sector is in essence sponsorship rather than giving. Sometimes sponsorship verges upon a financial transaction; cash for the charity virtually purchasing positive advertising for the company.

Companies often use sponsorship as part of their marketing 'mix', alongside other more conventional forms of advertising and PR. Well-targeted sponsorship can be extremely cost-effective for them, helping them to enhance their image. If they are targeting your church members, or the geographical area you serve in a particular drive for sales, sponsoring your activities can help them raise their profile directly among their target audience. If you are inclined to organize large events as part of your fundraising, you may be able to offer companies the chance to mix with clients and potential customers, offering them the opportunity to network to build good relationships.

However, inappropriate sponsorship is no use at all to them. They will not sponsor causes that have no relevance to their objectives, image, or target audiences. Indeed, they may not actually like your image – and you may have distinct reservations about theirs. They are sometimes aware that being seen to sponsor one cause may lead to floods of requests for sponsorship from other causes. The amount requested may be out of all proportion, or be timed towards the end of their financial year when the budget is all used up.

In any application for sponsorship, it is therefore vital to work out how the company can benefit from sponsoring you, and what tangible benefits you can deliver to them. Think of ways you could publicize their support, thus creating more positive PR for them. Add potential figures; how many would receive a newsletter, attend an event, pass a sign outside your building, and thus be influenced by the positive publicity you could offer? Can you be sure of positive coverage in the local press? As you come to actually apply, boost your credibility with letters of support. If you have had any positive local media coverage, make a collage display or a file of it to show them that you have a positive image to share. Use a personal contact to get your introduction if possible; one of your members may know an employee who would ask for you. This usually works far better than a 'cold' contact. Work out ways in which you can measure the success of your sponsorship, and try to build a relationship for further support in the future.

Gifts in kind
Some companies may just not have the money to give you a cash donation, however effective your sales pitch and however much they may wish to be associated with you. If they are on the verge of making staff redundant, it would be unpopular within the company to be seen to have money to spare on such things. However, they may still be able to support you in a number of other ways. Some have already been mentioned in the section on setting up a campaign office; gifts of office space, and redundant equipment can offer a lifeline to small charities and churches. They may be able to lay on training sessions or a brief placement in order to train your fundraiser with the administrative skills so necessary to the smooth running of a campaign.

A local grapevine could be operated through your members looking out e.g. for shops or businesses changing hands, relocating or downsizing, leaving good equipment to be scrapped. It is well worthwhile looking at what other physical resources your project might need in case items can be obtained as gifts in kind. Kitchen and electrical equipment can sometimes be given this way, perhaps when small hotels close or relocate. Sometimes everyone involved would be happier for equipment and furnishings to be put to a charitable purpose than to be scrapped. Occasionally factories may be able to spare a sample of their product more easily than cash, especially if they are seconds. Some businesses may have by-products that can be of use, e.g. planks, barrels and rope can form the basis of a huge range of development games for youth groups.

Sometimes a company may be going through a lean time, but be confident that things will pick up. Or they may be aware that some of their staff could benefit from a new challenge. In such circumstances, they may be prepared to consider seconding one of their staff to help you for a number of months. This can be of great help, particularly when seeking to adopt good practice within your administration. It will also help you to understand the corporate world to which you are applying, which may be very different from anything your institution has come into contact with before.

College example: Training for success

The Training for Success programme had its genesis some time ago in a five-year programme of funding from the government to various UK universities, called the Enterprise in Higher Education Initiative. Money was pumped into the university to kick-start various projects to help modern undergraduates acquire skills that would be useful both for them and for the country's economy when they entered the world of work. St John's participated in the scheme by developing a range of courses open to students from the whole university, for which they could enrol in the late afternoons and evenings – a little like evening classes in the wider community. St John's offered an administrative base and rooms for teaching free of charge. Students paid a registration fee for courses that in turn covered the cost of paying the course tutors a realistic rate for their teaching. The main cost that needed subsidy from the government funds was the salary of a part-time coordinator to make sure that the administration ran smoothly, and to cover the publicity costs – individually addressed brochures for each undergraduate in the university, mailed twice a year.

Problems inevitably arose when the five years of funding came to an end. Five years had provided time to develop the courses into a highly successful programme, with some 10 per cent of undergraduates taking part in courses each year. However, the college was not in a position to provide a subsidy itself to enable the courses to continue, and it seemed that the only hope for their survival lay in fundraising from external sources. With the good reputation the courses had established, and the extent to which the publicity brochures penetrated through the entire student body, it seemed that there might be real possibilities for sponsorship from companies that wished to gain a positive profile in the university.

Most of the major national accountancy firms recruit heavily in Durham, and many are regularly active in sponsoring sports clubs and other student activities in the university. It therefore made sense to target one of the national companies with a North-East presence. An introduction to the senior partner of one such company was secured with the help of a member of the college council. Having sent a written proposal for consideration, I was invited to meet the senior partner and one of his colleagues to discuss the extent of any support they might feel able to give.

Occurring as it did in the early months of my work as a fundraiser, I set off on this visit in fear and trepidation. I had the feeling that a decision to support us to some extent had already been made or the senior partner would not be giving up his time to see me. I would therefore be personally to blame if I came away empty-handed, and I would also be a comparative failure if the figure we eventually received was too small. Setting foot in the company's boardroom where our discussions took place was also a somewhat daunting experience, although I was kindly and courteously welcomed and put at my ease.

A time of detailed questioning followed. A previous responsibility I had held for the college was the coordination of the very courses I was now seeking to save for the future, which meant that I had detailed knowledge of the necessary facts and figures, a fact for which I was extremely grateful as the grilling continued. The result was substantial sponsorship of £3,000 per year for three years – a goodly sum indeed, but not enough on its own to secure the future of the courses. I remembered my fundraising consultant's advice, and as I left, thanked my hosts but explained the ongoing dilemma, and asked if they could themselves recommend any further sources of funding. This led to another introduction to a North-East firm of solicitors who a few weeks later also agreed to provide sponsorship, albeit at a lower level. These sums taken together provided just enough funding to allow the Training for Success programme to continue for another three years.

Points to remember

* Get your facts right – remember personnel change rapidly.

* Look for personal contacts wherever possible.

* Be aware of who might be looking for a better profile.

* Read the business news – who is doing well?

* Consider what you could offer in a sponsorship deal.

* Don't forget 'gifts in kind'.

* Build relationships for the future – boom times may come again!

14 Statutory sources

European Union funding

Love it or hate it, there is no doubt that the European Union's general budget is a substantial potential source of funding for many projects across its member states. This budget is made up of various taxes and levies on members, including a proportion of the gross national product of each constituent country.

Most money is channelled back into the member countries via the various Structural Funds, of which two may have particular relevance to local UK projects. The European Regional Development Fund (ERDF) aims to reduce regional imbalances, especially where there is industrial decline or rural poverty. It gives grants of sometimes substantial sums of money to capital projects. The European Social Fund (ESF) In contrast tends to give smaller amounts of revenue funding to support schemes that reduce long-term and youth unemployment, and to train the workforce for a changing job market.

Both ERDF and ESF funding will contribute up to 40 per cent or sometimes 50 per cent towards the costs of a particular project, looking to the bidders to lever in the rest of the necessary 'matching' funding to make up the total.

The EU has set various priority objectives, and any bid must fit within the criteria set for one or more of these. The economic development officer in your local authority will be able to advise you about successful projects in your locality and the criteria that apply to your region. The country is also covered by a network of European Information Centres, which will be able to supply basic information, as will your regional government office. They should also be able to advise you how to get details of the many other much smaller programmes of EU funding. These often have an element of exchange with other member states and presuppose that you have some established network of international contacts.

The Single Regeneration Budget

The Single Regeneration Budget (SRB) was set up by central government in 1994 to streamline the many sources and types of statutory funding available to agencies active in inner cities and other areas in serious need of economic regeneration. At the same time, the government offices referred to above were established in all regions of the country to administer this budget. Money from it is intended to complement existing funds from other sources, or to attract in new money from public, private or voluntary sources.

The hope is that by this unified approach, it will be possible to use funds far more strategically to make an impact for good in a particular area, drawing in a range of partners with good local knowledge to ensure that projects selected for support can make a qualitative difference to the local economy and the lives of the people living there. Such partners would normally include local authorities (LAs) and Training and Enterprise Councils (TECs). One partner, often the LA or TEC, would normally be expected to take the lead.

After the opening of a bidding round for a particular year, a number of months are available for local consultation and discussions, during which time the regional office may discuss outline bids with serious contenders for funding. Bids are then formally submitted for a certain date, after which the regional offices consider them and make recommendations to ministers, who reach the final decisions. After decisions have been announced, the regional offices may discuss the possibilities of carrying forward adapted proposals with partners of unsuccessful bids. In the meantime, the implementation of the approved bids begins approximately 12 months after the bidding round began, and the whole process rolls on for another year.

TECs

Training and Enterprise Councils are another comparatively recent innovation, set up to provide and stimulate further opportunities to help establish a modern flexible highly trained workforce to serve the country's economy. They receive funding from the government to carry out this purpose, and in turn have some funds to disburse to other smaller organizations. They have a number of staff specializing in different areas of training and regeneration, and are often significant partners in local and regional initiatives to secure money from the EU, SRB and other sources of finance. If your project is likely to provide opportuni-

ties for the disadvantaged to gain training and/or any recognized qualifications, it could well be worthwhile to talk through your plans with
your local TEC.

The Lottery

The National Lottery Etc. Act received Royal Assent in October 1993,
with the first draw being carried out 13 months later. In effect the
National Lottery actually provides several different potential sources of
funding, through the different boards; the original intention was to provide money for arts, sports and heritage projects, but lobbying from the
voluntary sector led to the inclusion of charitable 'good causes' as a
fourth element; at an even later stage in the planning the Millennium
Fund was added. Forty-nine per cent of the total income is distributed
between the five distributing bodies. Each is administered separately
with its own selection criteria and procedures, current guidelines concerning which are readily available.

The onus is on fundraisers to find projects that fit the published
guidelines. Competition for funding is greatest for money from the
National Lottery Charities Board; if a church-related project has a
strong arts- or sports-related emphasis and fits the criteria, the chances
of funding from those relevant distributing bodies is much higher.
There is now also a specific application procedure within the National
Heritage Board for churches seeking funds for their buildings.

If your church or organization is comfortable with the concept of
applying for Lottery funding, it is worth seriously investigating the possibilities. Once again, substantial funding from Lottery money will
require the raising of 'matching funding' before the Lottery funds can
be 'drawn down'. Failure to attract matching funding means the loss of
the award – a problem currently facing some of the high-profile multi-
million flagship awards already made.

Other statutory sources

The above-mentioned sources of statutory funding can sometimes yield
sums of six or even seven figures for major projects. However, there are
other, smaller sources for smaller projects, which may be more appropriate. For example, the government gives money each year to an
agency called 'English Partnerships', which was set up in 1994 with the
aim of promoting job creation, inward investment and environmental
improvement. They target their grants towards areas of particular need,

usually seeking to work in partnership with existing agencies. Their regional offices work closely with the government's regional offices that administer EU and SRB funding. They currently offer a simplified application procedure for smaller community-led projects requiring funding of up to £100,000.

The government also puts forward other smaller initiatives from time to time, as when it launched the 'Make a Difference' initiative, which included offering small grants to community groups through the 'Linking Communities' local grants programme. The basic concept was for community groups to be put in touch with each other in order to learn from each other, and to thus set up a network for mutual support.

Some community groups have been greatly helped by becoming linked to training providers in their area. Where training is an aspect of the project being developed by your church or organization, it could be fruitful to make contact with other funders such as further education (FE) institutions, who may be able to access Further Education Funding Council money to help with the costs. Links to formal training providers may mean that the basic training you can offer is able to be validated and certificated, so that your beneficiaries gain nationally recognized qualifications such as NVQs and GNVQs at various levels, or Royal Society of Arts or City & Guild qualifications. Sometimes accreditation of some kind can also be given to those who can prove they have achieved certain skills and competencies through the paid or voluntary work they are already doing for you, even if they left school with no exam passes to their name. These possibilities can help the individual greatly both in terms of personal self-esteem and in putting together stronger CVs in seeking employment in keeping with their true abilities.

Finding partners

Local authorities will have their own personnel with expertise and knowledge to share about possibilities and procedures in applying for statutory funds. They will also have a much wider perspective than you can hope to gain about the value of your project and its place in the overall strategy to help the people and prosperity of your area. It is worth building up good personal links with the right people serving in local and county councils at an early stage.

If your project fits well with larger applications that are already in process there can be real mutual benefit in joint applications, or even in letting a larger partner 'lead' a major bid on your behalf. Much of the weight of responsibility for filling in the all-important forms can then be lifted from your shoulders. Partners or contacts can also be extremely useful for you in providing letters of support to convince the assessors that your project will provide a much-needed service and fill a genuine gap not being met by others. This support can lead on to further practical help as your project gets under way, and your projected figures have to be replaced by real people and tangible impact on the local community.

Form-filling

The sheer size and complexity of the forms you are likely to face can be daunting and bewildering. However, there is no alternative to tackling them to the best of your ability. Before starting, it is wise to research your case to the full. For example, get copies of economic development strategies, corporate plans and annual reports of any bodies who might have something significant to say about the needs of your area. Other bodies are likely to have carried out research into the needs of your region, and their findings can be used selectively to demonstrate the need for your project.

If you do have sole responsibility for your application, it is worth seeking out any available training days to help you understand the process. Some forms are 'marked' on a simple ticks-in-boxes process, with the more ticks you amass giving the greatest likelihood of success. Knowing what happens to your form after you have posted it and how it is likely to be evaluated can help you maximize your chances of success. If you are required to estimate the numbers of beneficiaries of your project, do make sure that you can back these figures up with solid evidence before you submit the form, and be ready to defend the predictions you have made. Allowances will be made if the final reality does not quite match up to your hopes, as long as you can show good reasons for arriving at your figures.

College example: The ERDF grant

Funding from the European Regional Development Fund (ERDF) turned out to be a key element in the successful raising of quarter of a million pounds to open the Cross Gate Centre, a boarded-up former hospital wardblock in the city centre, for shared use with the commu-

101

nity. It was also by far the most demanding application we made in the whole campaign in terms of time, energy, research required and sheer stress.

We initially heard of the possibility of gaining such funding from a contact on our advisory group who had been helped to apply success-fully in another region for another type of project; they introduced us to a professional adviser, who agreed to visit the college free of charge and to assess our chances. His verdict was that we had a strong case for a successful application, and we duly applied for a project preview form to register our interest. The form was difficult to fill in at that stage for several reasons, partly because we were totally unused to this type of procedure, partly because the college as an institution didn't quite fit as a typical applicant for funds, and partly because even at that stage quite detailed predictions, e.g. about the number of jobs created or safe-guarded as a result of the project, were required.

Having submitted the preview form, the next stage was involvement in the local mutual selection procedure, the 'LAP Group', where other potential applicants decided on the relative priorities each project should receive. The system of LAP Groups is peculiar to the North-East, but works extremely well. Those projects receiving 'high' priority are likely to progress further, but this classification is not easy to achieve, as there are always far too many projects for available funds. We knew that anything less than high priority status would be likely to result in failure.

Going to the first LAP Group was an experience in itself; the college representatives gained a distinct impression that other bidders all knew each other well and were already aware of each other's work and plans. St John's College on the other hand was in a foreign environment, feel-ing at a disadvantage through not knowing the system at all. Aspects of our proposals came in for penetrating questioning – highlighting our lack of knowledge of what else was happening in the area. There was a particular understandable concern to avoid unwarranted duplication of facilities, and it was difficult to defend the Cross Gate Centre on these grounds given our lack of knowledge of other existing or planned pro-jects. The result was disappointing to say the least – failure to get that prized high priority status.

However, one great benefit did come out of what felt at the time to be a very negative experience. The city council's economic development officer saw definite potential in the scheme, and advised a slight change of direction for the building which would at the same time fit a real economic need in the area, give the Cross Gate Centre project a much clearer focus *vis-à-vis* EU funding, and allow us to take our place within an overall strategy for the area. The college agreed to incorporate the provision of several 'managed office units' into its plans for the building, giving low-cost accommodation for small businesses or voluntary groups, with shared access to telephones, fax, photocopier and some secretarial support. Our plans for conference/training facilities and a multi-media studio upstairs, integral to our proposed Centre for Christian Communication, were unaffected.

The establishment of cordial relations with the city council, and access through them to a network of interested local bodies, proved to be the key that unlocked the rest of the process. A subsequent LAP Group accorded the adapted project high priority; the government office in the North-East, which processes all applications, gave a great deal of helpful advice on the technicalities of filling in the full multi-page application form, and exactly a year on to the day from the college's North-East launch, we were able to announce a successful award of £109,760 for the Cross Gate Centre.

A beneficial side-effect of the hours spent on the application was the comparative ease with which other applications to charitable trusts could then be cut and pasted into shape. The supporting documents we assembled for the EU application also backed up our other applications; e.g. a detailed business plan for the first five years of operations, and a sheaf of letters of support from many sections of the local community. In the end we were able to raise a further £105,000 from several charitable trusts earmarked for the Cross Gate Centre, and to direct further 'unallocated' gifts to complete the total of necessary 'matching funding'.

The whole building was formally opened two years after the launch, the second campaign project to be seen through from initial vision to completion.

Points to remember

∗ Gather adequate information about the various types of statutory funding.

∗ Consider any implications, e.g. requirements for matching funding, limitations on future use of the property.

∗ Use any contacts for advice.

∗ Seek out possible partners.

∗ Research carefully to build your case.

∗ Make sure you can justify the statistics you provide.

∗ Discuss your application in draft form with experts before submitting.

---

15 Events

Organization of fundraising events is a high-risk and stressful part of fundraising. When things go smoothly they are merely exhausting, but when things go wrong they can become every charitable cause's worst nightmare. Careful planning is needed; tactful management of volunteers and a firm grasp of the basic objectives for each event are vital.

Usually the main aim of any event is to raise money, either at the event itself or later as a tangible result of it. However, there can be other important reasons: to raise the profile of your campaign locally or regionally; to enhance the image the public has of you, to make new friends or enthuse the ones you already have; to create good team spirit among your supporters; to enable those who cannot afford to give money to the campaign to have an alternative way to express their support; or even just to have fun and to reward your supporters.

The potential for disaster!

Having said that, any fundraising event that actually loses money is always a disaster in fundraising terms. Sometimes factors outside your control seem to conspire against you: your celebrity guest is unable to appear at the last minute; all your press coverage goes by the board because another issue blows up to take all the headlines; it rains; the caterer lets you down. Part of the reason that events are high-risk is that the larger (and therefore potentially more fruitful) your event, the more elements are outside your control. Careful planning can help to reduce the risk but can never quite remove it.

Plan your timetable

Each event benefits from having an organizing committee. It can be very helpful to all concerned to work on a universally agreed 'countdown to success', a timetable leading up to the event and including dealing with the aftermath – packing up, finances, thank-yous, etc. This basically lays down deadlines by which date all the various steps involved in organizing the event should be completed. Fall behind, and things may get critical! If you know someone from another church or charity that has first-hand experience of running a similar event, their help in planning your countdown to success will be extremely useful.

Launches

The public launch of your campaign provides a key opportunity to let the world know about your plans. It deserves months of preparation, as you will only ever have one chance to get it right. On the other hand a successful launch can give a tremendous boost to the campaign, and can also serve as a blueprint for further events as the campaign unfolds. Help from your campaign committee is vital. They may be in a position to help with some of the practicalities laid out in your countdown schedule – venue, timing, caterers, entertainment, tickets, publicity, etc., and they are crucial in the process of putting together the all-important guestlist. All your potential contacts in trusts, companies, church circles, plus local people of influence, should be invited. If you can obtain a special venue or guest celebrity with extra kudos this will help; for example the bishop's residence, if he supports what you are doing, or a local stately home, perhaps attended by a Christian celebrity.

The probability that your invitation will be taken seriously will be greatly improved if it is received in good time before busy diaries get filled up, and if someone the recipient knows and respects drops them a line a few days before your invitation arrives, forewarning them of the event, commending your cause, saying that they plan to be there, and encouraging them to attend too. This takes considerable organization but is worth the effort. It really is important to get as many people of influence together as possible, and for the occasion to have a positive effect on all who attend.

At a launch occasion, the emphasis probably should not be so much the generation of gifts of money on the night, but the creation of new friends and contacts who may be willing to make time for individual appointments to discuss ways to support you at a later date, and who may ultimately come through with much larger sums than a few pounds on the plate as they leave. Press coverage will enhance the impact of your launch. Press releases should stress both the value of your plans and the fact that X amount of money has already been raised towards your target.

High-profile events

Other periodic high-profile events during the course of your campaign may serve to maintain the momentum and keep you in the public eye. Again, planning months in advance is advisable, with clear targeting of potential guests, and careful costing of all aspects of the function. Calculate the catering costs per head, the publicity costs, any postage and telephone costs, printing of tickets, hire of the venue and not forgetting the cost of the time the fundraiser will inevitably spend making it all happen when he or she could have been working on other aspects of the campaign. Then make a conservative estimate of how many people you should be able to attract to your event. Divide the first figure by the second to arrive at the ticket price you will have to charge to have any hope of breaking even. Remember that some will be children, OAPs or 'concessions' who will be charged less, and build this in to your calculations.

Having followed these steps, you will be in a position to judge if the ticket price you have in front of you is realistic. Is the cost already so high that people in your area are unlikely to be able to attend? If so, you have a problem. Is there scope to increase it to give a better profit margin?

Then consider all the ways you can possibly think of to maximize the numbers attending. It is important to get your supporters committed to enthusiastic selling of tickets to all their friends and acquaintances so that you attain the maximum attendance possible!

Of course there are things you may be able to do to reduce the costs, so that more and more of the income from ticket sales becomes pure profit. Sponsorship immediately springs to mind; you may be able to attract local businesses or local branches of major companies to sponsor aspects of the event, including publicity and printing of tickets and programmes. If you can get your venue for free, and your special guests or entertainment to waive their fees too, another significant cost is removed. If you are able to assemble your own catering team, you should reduce the total needed even further – as long as they are capable of producing the quality and quantity you need. If you are careful not to tie up too much capital in stock you may be able to gain more income through merchandising, either handling this yourself or by allowing established traders to attend, charging them a fee or asking them to donate a proportion of their profits.

Small money-spinners

Many church projects will not aspire to a series of major fundraising events, but are almost certain to mobilize the troops for a succession of smaller fundraising events – coffee mornings, sales of work, sponsored events, etc. etc. These can provide a valuable way for those with creative gifts to contribute in kind as well as by cash giving. They illustrate that we can all contribute something positive whatever our circumstances. Often it is appropriate for a separate sub-committee to be set up to plan and run them.

However, a careful eye should be kept on the place they have in the overall scheme of things. Occasionally things can get a little out of hand, with a spirit of undue competition taking over between contributors! Sometimes serving the Church through good deeds becomes a substitute for serving the Lord in gratitude and faith, and can even become an excuse for non-attendance at worship. Sometimes far more money is expended in purchase of ingredients and materials for items for sale than is ever actually raised by the end product, which doesn't seem quite right if the main aim is to raise as much money as possible! Another serious point is that with small local events, it is likely that the same community of supporters will be expected to give over and over again. In an affluent area this may lead to an element of donor fatigue, but in a poorer area it may be a cause of real hardship, especially if this constituency has already been approached to commit themselves to sacrificial direct giving.

Gimmicks

There are many many different zany ideas for fundraising, and no doubt many more will occur to supporters of charitable causes seeking to have fun and raise money for their chosen causes. Several books are currently on the market which list fundraising ideas you might like to consider. Churches and Christian organizations will want to make sure that the gimmicks they choose to catch the public imagination are in accordance with their faith and witness. With a little creative thought an idea may arise that is new and fresh and which in some way may undergird the whole message of what you are trying to achieve. It may not in the first instance be a directly fundraising activity, but may illustrate in a vivid way the cause you are working for.

Practicalities

Much that is intensely practical will need to be sorted out as you plan for your event. Loos, parking, general access to the venue, disabled access, baby and toddler facilities, water, electricity, heating, lighting, acoustics, PA systems, the list goes on. Fortunately most churches are already likely to have some expertise in many of these areas, and should at least be able to come up with a list of the issues that will need to be thought through.

For many events, it can be an excellent idea to talk to the local authority at an early stage of your planning. They will be able to advise about their own policy for such events, and may be able to help you in a number of ways: by contributing some funding, providing publicity in their tourist guides, or allowing you to use council-owned land or buildings. The main local authority number in the telephone directory should be able to get you put through to the right department and an official who can help. Ask for a meeting if possible. Be prepared with as many details of your plans as possible. Take your budget along too and ponder carefully the implications of any contract you may be asked to sign for hire of venue or equipment – can you fulfil the conditions and afford it?

First aid support is provided free for events by arrangement with the Red Cross or St John Ambulance. They need plenty of advance warning and some idea of the likely numbers attending in order to give adequate provision.

Legal matters

Although it is not mandatory to ask permission of the Police to hold an event (unless there is some implication for public order), if you are expecting a significant number of people it is only sensible to do so. You should notify the divisional commander in writing as a first step, and you may find that a representative of the force may wish to attend your planning meetings or to be kept informed of developments. They will certainly need to know if you anticipate a large number of car-borne visitors, and will want to take steps to keep the roads clear. They will also want to know if you plan to sell alcohol; three months' warning and a special licence are necessary for this unless you will be using the bar of a building that is already licensed. An entertainments licence may be necessary if people are performing or if dancing is one of the activities (however, religious services and meetings are exempt!). Again, the relevant department within your local authority will be able to advise. They will also be able to tell you about local by-laws that may restrict what you can do when.

VAT

Be careful to make sure of the current VAT situation, up-to-date details of which can be obtained from HM Customs and Excise office. Basically, if your turnover as an organization is below a certain sum your event and your other operations will be exempt. However, if your turnover is above the designated threshold and your charitable events are seen as in any way competing with established commercial traders, putting them at a disadvantage because they have no choice but to pay VAT, you are likely to be liable. Exceptions are made for one-off or annual charity events for which one ticket price is charged, and at the other end of the scale, coffee mornings and bring-and-buy sales are deemed to present very little real competition and are also exempt. However, it is well worth seeking advice about your VAT status if you are at all unsure. Advice from skilled accountants is extremely valuable here, as in all aspects of your church or charity's finances.

Insurance

If anyone is injured in any way at an event you have organized, the consequences of facing a claim for damages could be crippling if you have not taken out basic public liability insurance. Even though you are not legally required to take it out, the relatively small premiums make sense. The more people attending and the more activities built into your event, the greater the need for cover. For unique events you may be able to find insurance companies that specialize in the particular activity featured. Be prepared for the cost to go up along with the risk associated with the activity, and expect to pay more for bungee jumping than for a vicarage tea party! It is also possible to take out insurance for All Risks, Money and Personal Assault, covering theft or damage to property associated with your event. An insurance broker would advise on all insurance matters. As with all policies it is imperative that you check the small print of your policy to learn the true extent of the cover you are purchasing, and any procedures which might invalidate it.

College example: The two public launches

St John's College decided that to have a major public launch would fit in well with the overall strategy of the campaign, giving an opportunity for a high-profile event to which a range of potential supporters could be invited. As a college with both a national and a regional role, the decision was actually made to have two launches, one in the North-East and one in London, maximizing the opportunity for raising the profile and letting everyone know that exciting new developments were happening at St John's.

Initial planning took place well in advance, and a special meeting of the full advisory group of the campaign was called to discuss the procedure we would adopt, and to begin the process of identifying potential guests. In London we were advised to set the time at around 6.30pm, with an assurance that guests would be able to leave without embarrassment by 8.00pm. This suited London lifestyles, allowing some people to arrive straight from work, and others to come before later evening engagements. The North-East launch, on the other hand, was set at 7.30pm, incorporating a concert programme, followed by a buffet and a chance to circulate. Each fitted the particular cultural situation and worked well on the occasion.

We were extremely fortunate in being offered two tremendous venues, which many guests would have found attractive and interesting in themselves. In London our patron the Archbishop of Canterbury offered us Lambeth Place, and in the North-East, former college ordinand Michael Turnbull opened Auckland Castle to us as one of his very first public appearances after his enthronement as Bishop of Durham. Both venues were prestigious, and their respective staffs were helpfulness personified in all the practical arrangements and the catering.

Probably the most strenuous week of the entire course of the campaign for me personally was the time when the launch invitations were sent out to the potential guests identified for us by our advisory group. It was complicated having two major events so close to each other. Around four hundred invitations were sent out to each launch, wherever possible a letter being sent to potential guests in advance by a respected friend who commended the college and endorsed the invitation. Timing was thus of the essence; some advisory group members wrote their own letters to their contacts, telling them to expect our invitations a few days later, while others asked us to produce their letters for them to subsequently top and tail and send out. Sometimes more than one advisory group member knew the same guest and decisions had to be made as to who should be the prime contact. Other decisions included whether to write to people at their home or their work addresses, and whether or not it was appropriate to invite their wives. The invitations needed individually inscribing in italic script, and the envelopes were too big to go through our computer printer *en masse* and also needed individual printing. Much midnight oil was burned!

A great deal of attention was given to the programme through the evening, with the college's students given a prominent place from which to exhibit their many talents. At Auckland Castle several gifted individuals contributed to a small programme of musical items, and at each event a small strings orchestra provided beautiful background music as guests circulated and visited the exhibitions. Central to each evening was a short presentation by the principal, David Day, whose own communication skills came to the fore magnificently. We had decided not to overtly ask for money directly on either evening, though the mechanism to give was there should guests wish to avail themselves of it. The main thrust of the evening was actually to seek a time commitment from guests; to ask them to be willing to give a subsequent half hour to talk through the campaign projects and practical ways in which they might be able to help.

After the presentation, guests were invited to stay for light refreshments. Student volunteers circulated with drinks and trays of hors d'oeuvres, others being deputed to engage guests in conversation, stationed strategically close to particular exhibition stands that related to the different strands of the campaign of which they had personal knowledge. Many guests, especially in London, were charmed to meet real students in the flesh! Each launch continued well past the designated time for ending, with many interesting and enthusiastic conversations taking place. Snippets of information were recorded later in a debriefing session, and filed for further use.

Each launch was pronounced a resounding success, with around 100 guests at each. The students were wonderful ambassadors for their college, and the principal, David Day, successfully communicated the essence of the campaign to those present, ably assisted by the campaign chairman, Roger Kingdon. Many of the subsequent larger donations could be traced directly back to the impact of these occasions on those present, and many good friends were created. The investment in time, energy and personal stress was high, but the results were well worthwhile. The costs involved were amply repaid as the following weeks and months went by.

Points to remember

* Events always entail a risk!

* Plan your 'countdown for success' well in advance, leaving time margins for error.

* Share the workload by using a committee.

* Approach the planning carefully to maximize attendance.

* Pay attention to practicalities; accept all the help you can muster.

* Choose gimmicks carefully.

* Talk to the local authority.

* Take advice about legal liability, VAT and insurance.

---

16 Media relations

Many church people have a deep suspicion of the media in all its forms, and an expectation that to put information about their activities into the hands of the press is to ask for trouble. However, as in many spheres of life, behind the headlines and images we receive there are individual people just doing a job. Christians are also in the communication business through the very nature of their faith – we actually have much in common with those who gain their livelihood through it! The title of this chapter suggests that it is indeed possible to build a relationship with reporters, copywriters and editors.

I would argue that it is worth taking time to cultivate such relationships. Very few churches have a member who takes on responsibility for media relations, even if this involves purely issuing lists of dates and times of services. However, it can be no bad thing to establish clear links and channels of communication with the media, particularly with the local press and radio stations. This is true for the everyday life of the institution as well as for the special occasions where you would love to see a double-page spread on your fundraising work. Every scrap of coverage you receive will be read by many more individuals than ever darken church doors on a Sunday, and will serve to help build up an overall image of your institution and your ministry among local people. There are a number of ways to set about creating positive links, each taking time, care and a strategic approach in order to convey the information you want to your public.

What is 'news'?
Anything that is new is news! Having said that, you do need to put a bit of thought into exactly what aspects of your community life are newsworthy. All the hard work in the world fostering links with the media will not lead to the publication of essentially boring material with little

relevance to the target audience. It is worth considering the most interesting slant or angle you could use to approach your news item. People's personal experience can be interesting – new staff members or volunteers, especially if they have an unusual story to tell or an unusual talent to share. So can new activities undertaken by your church or organization, especially if relevant to the community served by the newspaper – a children's holiday club complete with photos, an old people's lunch club, even a men's breakfast. Special events in your calendar can merit coverage, as can anything you do linked to a public personality or celebrity. Watch out for other topical subjects in the news – you may be able to get coverage for one of your activities on the back of another story already receiving attention. Your approach must be imaginative, never dull.

Media releases

Local newspapers usually have only a small staff, and you may find that by sending in appropriate press releases you begin to get regular coverage in them quite quickly, effectively giving you free publicity. There are a few basic rules to follow: use single sides of A4, typed up using double-spaced lines. Leave wide margins for the journalist to add his or her own notes. Keep your text brief, free of jargon and formatted in snappy short sentences. Think of the questions the readers or listeners are likely to want answered and include these answers in the press release. Try to find an attention-grabbing first sentence, leading into factual material – who? what? when? where? why? Include a quote from your leader or respected community representative. Make sure you clear the content of your press release with all concerned before you send it off.

Send in releases little and often, each focusing on a single distinct event or report. Read the papers you send releases to regularly to get a feel for their style and the kind of issues they like to cover, and write your press releases to complement these. Always include a contact name and number for the reporter to ring up for further information, and make sure that whoever answers that phone is both well briefed and competent to answer further questions accurately. Once you have had one or two conversations with a local reporter and the relationship is well on the way, you can then send your releases to him or her by name. They in turn will be more likely to turn out to cover your special events, or may pass on promising subjects within the paper, perhaps to the feature editor for an in-depth article at a future stage.

An awareness of appropriate timing can be useful too; if you time your releases for a Sunday, bank holidays or between Christmas and New Year there may be less 'news' passing through the newsroom and your story has more chance of being selected. If you are sending a release to a weekly or monthly paper, aim to make contact the day after the day they went to press, as this is often a quiet time. A good action photograph accompanying your article can also help secure coverage. If you have a particularly special event, it may be worth putting together press packs for the local media, including a press release, photographs and background briefing information. You could even consider organizing a press conference and photo opportunity; holding these in the middle of the morning suits the daily pattern of work of most newspapers.

Keep your press cuttings

Save copies of all the coverage you receive, and build a dossier or file of it all; this could be kept in a loose-leaf file in the church's foyer or organization's reception area to be leafed through by casual visitors. Collages of clippings concerning aspects of church life can be made and photocopied to demonstrate the strength of your links with the community and the good profile you have, encouraging sponsorship opportunities and supporting other applications you make.

Newsletters

It is of course quite possible to write your own material to keep your campaign in the public eye. However, it is worth considering the implications of taking this step before you start. Are you sure there are enough people out there who need to know your progress to justify the time and effort you will have to put in? And will you have enough 'news' to fill it? Sometimes it is easy to assemble enough material to make a strong first edition, but by the time you get to issue number three or four, news can be decidedly hard to come by. If you pace your material well, you will find that over time newsletters can give a good insight into your work for potential supporters and funders. Disseminate copies of your newsletter to as many potential supporters as you can, both in the local community and among potential funders further afield.

Your newsletter may just take the form of two sides of A4 produced in-house, or may be a glossy production, professionally printed, with colour photos and layout. Cost and size of circulation may dictate which course you follow. However, certain principles will apply throughout. Think through who it is aimed at and what the overall message is that it is trying to convey before writing the text. The style needs to be appropriate to you as a church or institution. Put real thought into attractive layout that is easy on the eye; if you do not have access to expert advice, get hold of as many different newsletters from other organizations as you can, and decide what you think works. Good photographs will enhance its attractiveness and the number of people who will read it. Interviews will give a human perspective and angle to the campaign. Try to present facts, figures and statistics in visual ways whenever possible – graphs, bar charts, pie charts and the like are much easier to grasp than dry columns of figures.

Radio coverage

Releases sent to radio stations follow the same principles as those to the press – minus the photographs for obvious reasons! Reporters may follow up your release by getting in contact and arranging a live or recorded interview either at the radio station, your office or at the site of the project. Try to add atmosphere to the context if you can; remember that words and sounds have to paint pictures in the imaginations of the listeners, and relevant background noises can help by adding atmosphere. Practice thinking and speaking in 'soundbites' – brief sentences encapsulating the message you want to get over in under thirty seconds.

If you have the courage and a quick wit, more and more local radio stations have phone-in shows where viewers are encouraged to ring and express their views. If sensitively done, this could provide another avenue for free publicity. It goes without saying that a cool head is needed, and wisdom to use appropriate words in an appropriate context – beware of soundbites that might come back to haunt you, taken out of their original context. Unless explicitly authorized to speak on behalf of a church or organization, it should be made clear that the views expressed are personal.

TV

It may even be possible to attract television cameras to a high-profile event, such as the opening of new facilities or the visit of a celebrity. However, more and more camcorder material is finding its way into local news coverage these days, and if you have an enthusiastic amateur video maker at hand you may even find that you are able to provide some usable coverage of your event. If you are able to supply the film, you control the images actually broadcast to a much greater degree, which has to be a great bonus. With the coming of cable television and the likely generation of hundreds of new local TV channels in the future, all competing for low-budget content, this kind of material is likely to be screened more often.

Receiving a bad press

One scenario where your hard work cultivating a positive relationship with the local media can reap enormous dividends is in the event of some disaster or controversy leading to a 'bad press'. Newspapers are in business to sell copies and give the public what they want, and sadly bad news can so often lead to higher sales than good news. Having friends in the media can sometimes allow for a damage limitation exercise to be carried out; perhaps a story with damaging effects can be relegated from the front to an inside page, with a more sympathetic treatment of the issue; perhaps a quote from a church representative can be included to balance up the coverage, or a letter laying out your own perspective be published in the next edition. Forewarned can be forearmed, and to know what is likely to be printed or broadcast can allow you to take sensible steps to redeem the situation. In extreme cases, the best policy can be to explain the whole story fully to all your members and supporters, issue a press statement after prayer and due consideration, and ask all those who support you to refer all journalists' enquiries to the statement, or to one or two named individuals through whom all press comment will be focused. Thankfully, although the heat can be extreme while it lasts, the media are ever hungry for new stories and new dramas, and their attention will pass.

College example: Radio interview about the Cross Gate Centre

Establishing links with the media can sometimes lead to requests for speedy action! Local radio stations had given some airtime to the original launch of the development campaign, and had been continually included in the list of media contacts receiving press releases about our progress. One spring morning the college development office received a call from a local radio station which had received one such press release, which had announced that contractors would be starting work that very day on the wardblock building that was to become our Cross Gate Centre. Could we provide someone to be interviewed that day on the subject, to be broadcast the next morning?

As luck would have it, I was already engaged for the day and could not help. Our principal David Day was out of Durham. The onus was on my assistant Lois, newly appointed as part-time public relations officer, to put something together within a couple of hours.

Her first achievement was to locate the campaign chairman, Roger Kingdon, and to establish that he could be available as a senior college representative to front the interview, which meant that there would be at least two voices and perspectives to draw on when the interviewer arrived. A few further phone calls elicited the facts that (1) it would be possible for the interview to take place on site at the Cross Gate Centre as the contractors worked around them, and (2) that the centre's first tenant in the managed office space units, the Churches Regional Commission in the North-East, would be available for comment. The commission was already camping out using minimal office facilities upstairs as the contractors created their permanent accommodation downstairs. The director Chris Beales was an old hand at coping with the media, and so we were sure that he would find something positive and original to say, in his typical infectiously enthusiastic manner. In a very short time it seemed that a worthwhile piece of radio was in the making.

When the reporter from the radio station arrived, prior preparation meant that the various elements fell into place very quickly with the minimum of wasted time or effort. Sound effects were all around, to give atmosphere to the piece. Roger Kingdon arrived to be interviewed strolling through the building, as hammering, drilling and general mayhem echoed around him. Then it was over to Chris Beales, who had brought along a local lad on work experience using computers with the commission as part of the employment training he was receiving from YMCA Training (who themselves were renting a separate wing of the building from the college). This added another perspective, and some local interest, to the piece. Finally Lois herself was brought in to wind it up. The result – a neat radio item of some three and a half minutes that was broadcast at several points during the day, across Teesside, Durham and Newcastle.

Points to remember

* Take every opportunity to cultivate the press.

* Think carefully about what is newsworthy.

* If you have good material, try to release media releases regularly to build up an awareness of your cause.

* Keep a file of all the coverage you get.

* Build personal contacts within the media.

* Help them if you can by providing knowledgeable contributions.

* Use your contacts to limit damage if you get bad publicity.

---

17 Merchandising and trading

Small-scale merchandising

Merchandising of some kind can provide a valuable back-up to mainstream fundraising. Items made or purchased can be sold on to supporters of the campaign or the general public at a profit, the proceeds going to swell the total being raised. The money thus obtained is 'unallocated', with no strings attached – always the best kind of income for a fundraiser to receive. It sounds ideal. However, as ever there are practicalities to be sorted out before merchandising on any scale should be contemplated. Adequate investment of time, money and resources is needed for merchandising to reap proper dividends. There is an element of risk involved in even relatively small-scale schemes.

First, it is wise to examine the practical logistics. Do you have secure storage space to keep a range of items in stock? Do you have the people available as volunteers to sell the merchandise, and the expertise to manage the scheme appropriately? Do you have enough outlets to generate a reasonable number of sales? Will the public want to buy your merchandise because it is genuinely marketable, or will you be relying once more on your circle of known supporters to give their money to make the scheme work? How much money will you have to lay out in order to eventually make a profit? Do you have that kind of money to hand?

A variety of companies are already active in the voluntary sector, who are always looking for further outlets for their wares, and who would be pleased to talk to you. They often major on the kind of small items that would sell well on a church bookstall – pens, mats, keyrings, badges, cards. Companies like Webb Ivory have a long history of working with charities, using agents to sell through catalogues, with a percentage on each sale going to the charity of the agent's choice.

Volunteer enterprises

Merchandising can, of course, be much closer to home. There may be a homegrown skill or talent within your church or supporting group that has fundraising potential. Photographic or artistic skills can lead to a range of pictures, cards or posters being produced. Depending on the quality sought, colour photocopies of various sizes can now be run off and marked up to be sold at a profit without the need to carry a huge stock. Calendars are another possibility. Tabletop scanners are becoming more widespread, where an image can be scanned in to a computer and printed straight out on a colour printer. Cookbooks of tried and tested personal recipes can also be a good money-spinner – though an eye needs to be kept on infringement of copyright: recipes should not be lifted straight from commercial cookbooks!

Coffee shops, etc.

Some churches and organizations have branched out into coffee shops or drop-in centres, often to provide a service to the local community as much as to generate income. Homemade baking and refreshments are served, and the proceeds used to underpin a particular project or as an unallocated contribution to church funds. As with all business ventures, an adequate business plan should be drawn up before embarking on such a scheme, to be sure that all the costs have been anticipated, that there really is a market out there for the service, and that enough people are seriously committed to the concept to give it long-term viability. There is often a substantial measure of sacrificial giving of time, effort and money in such enterprises, without which they would not be sustainable, and if this is the case it should be openly acknowledged from the start.

Charity shops

High street shop premises given over to a variety of charities are now a common sight in our towns and cities. Most sell donated secondhand goods at reasonable prices and are staffed mainly or completely by volunteers. Most can claim substantial tax concessions and rate relief, as long at the profits are used for charitable purposes. From the point of view of the Charity Commission as well as the Inland Revenue, as long as these shops are not buying and selling new goods it is generally agreed that they are not so much trading as taking the opportunity to convert items donated as gifts in kind into cash for their cause.

However, once such shops begin to introduce a proportion of new goods into their range the situation may change, and it is well worth taking expert up-to-date advice if this is contemplated.

Charity shops bring obvious benefits in terms of a stream of income that can be used by the church or charity to fund its work, with no strings attached. However, they also serve as a powerful visual aid of the involvement of your institution in the everyday real world. Many people will walk past your window each day, glancing at it as they pass. Some may drop in casually, sometimes handing in donations rather than buying. Others may call because they want to be put in touch with your organization or church, because they have basic enquiries, seeing you as a point of contact.

The atmosphere and feel of such shops is very important, as they will convey to passers-by the ethos of the cause the shop is supporting. If it is grubby and dingy, and the staff make no real effort to help customers or be friendly, the image conveyed will be negative; if thought and care is put into presentation and decor and the staff are eager to be of help, the impression given will be far more positive.

The goods that are received for sale should be rigorously sorted, and the first priority is to remove those that would quite frankly only repel shoppers from visiting your premises again. Sub-standard stock will only lower your reputation, and can still raise a little cash for you if sold on for scrap. Buttons and trimming may be removed and separately bagged for sale before you despatch rejected garments; sometimes fabric can be re-presented, perhaps for patchwork or making stuffed toys, perhaps with the shop then offering an outlet for such informal cottage industry.

Remember that certain articles cannot legally be resold – used crash helmets, furniture that does not conform to modern fire safety regulations, spectacles. Some may be too risky – electrical equipment that cannot be tested, old gas heaters. If in doubt, contact the local trading standards officer.

VAT and tax issues

Of course, a couple of brief paragraphs can do little to convey the complexities and pitfalls for the unwary in the British tax system. It is extremely important that any church or charity gets expert advice before embarking on the major commitment involved in any commercial activity. This is especially true of activities selling directly to the public, whether charity shops or coffee shops, as more and more mainstream high street traders are complaining vociferously about unfair advantages for charities. Those running the activity must ensure they know the relevant laws and guidelines for good practice. Good advice from solicitors and accountants who know the ins and outs of charity law and the convoluted tax and VAT regulations is crucial. Trustees need to be certain of their own liabilities, as do those who sign any lease agreement on the organization's behalf. Getting tax, especially VAT, wrong can have serious implications, and if not detected immediately the backlog can prove crippling to a small operation. On the other hand, money can sometimes be saved, sometimes to the tune of substantial amounts, by wise attendance to the regulations.

The use of volunteers

The handling of any sort of merchandising operation implies the use of at least a small team of staff to manage the whole process; for churches and other small operations this is likely to mean recruiting an ongoing succession of willing helpers. Using volunteers has great advantages, but can also bring problems in its wake. It is best for all concerned to think through the nature of the help needed and whose gifts and abilities are best fitted for selling, handling money and dealing with the public.

Volunteers work for charitable causes for a number of reasons. Most will feel a sense of the importance of 'the cause'. Some will have sufficient means not to have to rely on paid employment, others may see a spell of voluntary work as a stepping-stone back into the labour market. Some may be lonely and crave company, others may find a sense of self-worth through a job which to them has real value. It is important that whatever volunteers are looking for, they get some sense of satisfaction in return for their contribution, and that they feel involved and needed. It is also important that no one person gains undue dominance and that all function as a harmonious team. Careful management is needed, and a clear understanding of what is expected of them and the limits of their role. An initial job description listing expectations and mutually agreed standards can help and be referred back to if problems do arise.

College example: Prints and notelets

Soon after the campaign launches, St John's College received an offer of help from a former student, who had retired from full-time Christian ministry, and had developed a considerable talent for watercolour painting. Before he retired, he had been a school chaplain, and had given the rights of several of his watercolours of the school grounds to the school, which was then able to raise money through sales of prints and notelets produced from the original paintings. He offered to do the same for the college.

This was a wonderful offer, and one that we accepted with alacrity. The paintings were duly supplied: two popular views of Durham itself and two of the college. A limited edition of the prints were produced and signed and numbered by the artist, augmented by packs of eight notelets with envelopes – two of each print per pack. A firm of printers whose workmanship was known to the artist was used to produce these, to ensure a satisfactory quality. The original outlay was in the region of £2,000 for the printing work; a considerable sum but one that we saw as a good investment in the long term.

Fliers advertising the prints were produced at the same time, and were included in our regular alumni mailings to former students. The result was pleasing – a steady flow of orders for both prints and notelets which the development office duly processed. However, we did notice a sharp decrease in the number of small individual donations to the development campaign at the same time. It seemed as though many people who might have given something to us as a small straight donation instead chose to purchase a few packs of notelets. An order form for future purchases was always included when despatching the order, and some especially keen supporters come back for more regularly.

We did experience considerable problems with the mailing of framed prints to alumni, with a distressing number of prints arriving at their destinations broken or damaged, despite using packaging as recommended and supplied by the Post Office. Equally disappointing was the amount of compensation forthcoming for these cases, which in no way covered the costs involved. As problems persisted, we eventually worked out an arrangement with a small local picture framing company who now frame prints for us to order, and also handle the delivery, for very little extra cost. This removed what had become a considerable pressure and worry from our shoulders, and appears to be working well.

Two years on at the time of writing, this small merchandising operation has comfortably covered its costs and provides a slow but steady stream of income. Considerable stocks remain which will in time add extra profit with each successive sale. We have found a retail outlet with some sales directly to tourists in the summer through a local café that hangs the prints and sells them on our behalf. However, the amount of storage space needed and the ongoing administrative work involved have made us cautious about venturing into other areas of merchandise. We would think very carefully before tying up more significant amounts of capital in different kinds of stock, and carrying all the risk of any failure ourselves. If we had a wider range of marketing outlets no doubt sales would be turning over more quickly. However, each year a new generation of students enters the college, creating new opportunities for sales as they purchase them as mementoes or proud parents buy them as graduation gifts. In time this operation will raise a sum comfortably into five figures for the campaign – an extremely good return for our initial investment.

Points to remember

* Consider the practicalities: storage, manpower, sales outlets.

* Consider buying into existing merchandised products.

* Look around your organization for existing income-generating talents.

* Formulate a business plan before you start, to make sure it is all worth it.

* Make sure your merchandising operation reflects your ethos.

* Expert advice is worth it even if it costs!

* Organize your volunteers with care.

---

18 The ongoing cycle

Maintaining momentum

Many fundraising campaigns find it harder to achieve the second half of the target sum they have set themselves to raise, even when they have experienced some spectacular success in raising the first half. This is not helped by the all too common tendency of some actual targets to increase inexorably as time goes by. By and large, this has been the experience of the St John's College Development Campaign. The behind-the-scenes preparation and fundraising before the launch went well. The launches themselves led to a number of fruitful contacts and some substantial donations. However, a couple of years down the line, the stream of income began to slow down. Some of the more obviously attractive likely potential major donors had been approached, some-times for more than one project in succession, and had either decided to give or declined. It was too soon to approach them yet again. The easiest sources and the easiest causes to raise money for had thus been dealt with, leaving us to turn our attention to the less likely sources in order to fund the less popular projects.

When a campaign runs out of steam a little, it can be very demoral-izing for all concerned. However, there are a number of ways of tack-ling the problem, as these things very often run in cycles. The secret is to adapt your strategy to kick-start things into life again. This is one of the reasons why paying attention to PR can be so worthwhile. Main-taining a good profile locally gives you a much stronger base from which to canvass continuing support, especially when changing empha-sis from working on a few big applications from national sources, to approaching a larger number of smaller sources, often local, for smaller amounts. It is easier to argue for further support from a position of demonstrable success than desperation to avoid failure. Use any small step along the way to maintain the impression that things are still moving – major donations, the contractors moving in, the completion of each phase, the opening of the project, its first piece of work, its first anniversary, annual reports. It is always an advantage to be able to fundraise for something that is new, innovative or filling a special niche in some way. Even once a project has begun, it is still possible to fundraise for a specific piece of work or activity within it. This may still allow you to claim a measure of innovation and uniqueness, into which an element for overheads and depreciation for the whole operation can legitimately be costed.

Evaluation

The importance of evaluation both of your fundraising strategy and the success of the projects you are fundraising for is significant here. At the beginning of the whole fundraising process you set targets, estimating measurable outcomes and costs, making them as realistic as you could at the time. Are these being achieved, exceeded, or is reality falling short of your predictions? What factors, unknown at the time, have influenced these variations? What is there to learn from it all? How have others tackled a similar situation? If you are falling short of your expectations, there may be good reasons for this. Make sure you know what they are; trusts and other funders will appreciate feedback about your progress, and to be able to explain the variances will help them understand the situation and will maintain your credibility in their eyes. It may even mean that they are willing to consider giving added support to your project, as long as you can reassure them that they will not be throwing 'good money after bad'.

Donor fatigue

However, beware of creating 'donor fatigue', where donors just get thoroughly fed up of your regular unremitting stream of requests for further help. Both at the level of major trusts and in fundraising from local people around your community, there is a certain threshold of tolerance which you exceed at your peril. Many trusts will not consider further requests from the same organization within a year, sometimes longer. Many neighbourhoods can cope with a series of fundraising events for one special cause for a short concentrated length of time, but increasing ingenuity may be needed to maintain interest and commitment. Quite simply, people may get sick of hearing about you, and consequently become resistant to your requests for money.

Different timescales for different targets

It can be very helpful to look at the types of fundraising income you are attempting to generate, with an eye to how quickly the money is likely to come flowing in from these different sources. Your aim should be to ensure as regular a stream of income as possible. Some types of income are one-off and relatively speedy; gift days, collections and events are likely to generate money quickly. However, the wheels within trusts and companies can appear to turn agonizingly slowly and there is nothing you can do to hurry them up; they work to their own established timescale. It can take months for the money to come through from trusts, even if your application is successful. Merchandising operations are likely to generate a constant small flow of income, though an eye needs to be kept on cashflow and associated expenditure, e.g. the buying in of stock. Legacy promotion is definitely a long-term strategy, though one that undoubtedly yields dividends in time. The average length of time from initiating a legacy programme to the first income is measured in years. Think about the kind of amounts you need, and the speed at which you need them, and concentrate your efforts accordingly.

An exit strategy

Most fundraising campaigns have a very definite beginning, lifetime and conclusion. Churches and smaller organizations have the capacity to mount an effective high energy operation for a certain time, seeking commitment from staff, volunteers and donors that is so intense that it cannot possibly be maintained long term. Volunteers are often recruited for a certain length of time, and throw themselves into fundraising knowing that no one expects them to keep up the pace indefinitely.

From the beginning, an eye should be kept on how to wind up the fundraising operation, to exit with grace from the fundraising merry-go-round. Sometimes those involved can experience a real sense of bereavement as the work winds down, and the sense of involvement in a team, giving them value, purpose and a sense of achievement is lost. It may indeed be appropriate to keep a small-scale fundraising operation going, perhaps focusing more on maintaining a lower level of income, maintaining relationships with key individual donors and trusts, and overseeing a small continuing merchandising operation and a regular calendar of events, alongside more traditional stewardship oversight and the monitoring of covenants.

Sometimes the conclusion of the actual project can create a vacuum, leaving the beneficiaries feeling more abandoned than before the project started. Issues like this can usually be predicted and appropriate pastoral care drawn in. Sometimes a pilot programme or short-term project that has proved its value can continue on a different basis, either through volunteers, or with elements of partnership with other bodies, attracting elements of statutory funding or funding from other agencies. The project may be able to take on contract work, being paid for the services it delivers. The emphasis often shifts from capital start-up costs derived from your fundraising activities to the securing of revenue funding to sustain continuing work year by year. Whatever happens, even if it was always understood that the project would wind up as income from fundraising decreases, ensure that the lessons learned from the project are recorded and fed back into the life of the church or the parent institution. Such lessons should never be wasted.

Planning for the future
It is worth taking time to record every detail of your fundraising campaign meticulously, to allow the threads and networks of contacts to be easily picked up once again in the future. Those charged with the responsibility of fundraising for your institution in the future will bless you for it. While it is sensible for all concerned to rest between fundraising campaigns, to avoid donor fatigue and exhaustion among your volunteers, and to allow you to consolidate and integrate the achievements of your last fundraising initiative, there is nothing to stop you praying and planning around the issues of having another fundraising push after a break. It can be easier the next time around – you learn so much through the actual doing of fundraising, and you will have many more contacts to use as a starting-off point.

The cycle can repeat itself many times over, as you move from vision to planning, from action to achievement, from evaluation to new vision. It is an exciting path to follow, and can lead to wonderful achievements from tiny mustard seed beginnings. Visions can be dangerous and unsettling things to live with, but as the Book of Proverbs tells us, where there is no vision the people perish.

College example: The garden room
Rereading the text of earlier chapters has made me realize just how fortunate St John's College has been to experience a measure of success in so many aspects of the development campaign. However, just in case

you get the impression that it has all been too easy for us, I would like to conclude the series of examples drawn from our real life experience in St John's College by sharing an episode that has not been quite so positive, and which has forced us to address the issue of when it is right to actually give up our efforts.

Much of our success has been focused on projects which, while extremely valuable and worthwhile, and a true reflection of our ethos and mission, have not directly addressed the college's continual need for better facilities for our students on our original site. Some time after the campaign launch, an introduction to a particular charitable trust through a former student who knew an administrator there led us to consider adding an additional major building project to our portfolio. The building in question would serve students of both Halls, by providing modern lecture space for ordinands by day and social space for undergraduates by night, with the possibility of an additional venue for courses and special lectures for the public thrown in. Essentially a simple square building ten metres by ten, the college architect designed a graceful edifice to fit on the lawns overlooking the riverbanks to the rear of the main range of buildings, with generous use of glass and wood to 'bring the garden into the room and the room into the garden', minimizing the environmental impact and maximizing its aesthetic appeal. It has to be said that a major factor leading us to incorporate the project to build this 'Garden Room' as part of the campaign was the unlooked-for possibility of substantial funding from the trust. Our heads had definitely been turned.

Timescales were always tight because of the need to build the whole building in the course of the twelve-week summer vacation, to avoid disruption of college life during term time. Other constraints were imposed by this trust's own internal timetable which was rigidly adhered to, and which could not be hurried. As weeks turned to months it became clear that we would miss the first year's deadline. Costs rose inexorably, but by a combination of reallocation of existing donations, sale of property and an eventual generous award of £20,000 from the trust, it was decided that building work should commence the next summer. The work was put out to tender accordingly.

It was only when these tenders from contractors were actually received that it was realized that the costs had rocketed once again, coming in way over the estimates of the quantity surveyor. After lengthy discussions in the most difficult meeting of the entire campaign, the executive committee felt that the new costings, which now came in at well over £1,000 per square metre of building, could no longer in all conscience be seen to represent good value for money, and that therefore the project should be abandoned. We had got it wrong.

The trust which had awarded us the £20,000 allowed us a substantial period of time to find a suitable alternative, and five different options elsewhere in the college or nearby were examined closely, but there were insuperable problems with each scheme. The needs the project was designed to address were real and remain pressing. Finally we relinquished the money, and abandoned the scheme in any shape or form. A bitter pill to swallow, but a lesson learned. My advice – think everything through carefully before letting the possibility of money drive your projects.

Points to remember

* Remember you will need to rethink your strategy if income dries up before you have reached your target.

* Keep your profile positive with good PR.

* Consider new aspects of existing projects to raise funds.

* Evaluate your progress constantly.

* Beware of asking too many people for money too often.

* Plan a range of fundraising methods to draw in income at different rates.

* Wind up your current campaign and project thoughtfully.

* Seek renewed vision for your next campaign.

PART THREE **PRINCIPLES**

19 Image versus truth

Selling

All fundraising is to a certain extent a kind of selling. We are selling the cause we are working for, with special attention to the benefits that will result from donations and gifts. Selling implies the need for market research, which helps us to produce targeted advertising to promote our product. Given this truth, there may be lessons to learn and new insights to gain from the market activity that goes on around us all the time, and in which we are immersed in twentieth-century society. This may reveal deeper issues to be teased out for fundraisers seeking to work to the highest ethical standards.

It is a fact that a far larger proportion of the population is personally involved in regular purchasing than in regular selling. Most of us feel comfortable about buying groceries and other necessities of life, but comparatively few of us would be comfortable hawking our wares door-to-door for a living or working as market traders selling directly to the public. Indeed, for many, selling is a suspect activity, perhaps a little foreign to the reserved British psyche. Even in church life, it can be difficult to get enough volunteers to sell copies of the parish magazine or collect on doorsteps for Christian Aid Week.

For Christians, part of the reason may lie in a subconscious reaction to the fact that selling usually occurs in a negative context in the Bible, for example the caustic strictures of prophets such as Amos. However, we should remember that the sociological context in Old Testament times was very different, arising out of a largely self-sufficient agrarian culture, where hard currency was not as important as today, with the highly sophisticated market economy we now live in. Some may also see a potential conflict between our inclination to protect ourselves and our future by surrounding ourselves with the material goods we purchase, and the biblical injunction to live by faith.

Using marketing methods

Some selling is highly personal in nature. Sales representatives cover specific patches and build up relationships with their clients over the years. Some of their success is linked directly to their own credibility with their customers, and to the track record of customer service they provide. A good rep thinks about the wants and needs of the customers, being patient, available and hard-working. All these qualities translate easily into the fundraising context.

Selling in a wider context leads on to advertising and marketing. The objective here is slightly different and has a much wider context than purely personal selling. The aim is to create or raise the profile of the product and to make sure that when people come across it, it triggers off positive associations in their minds. Advertising can also be used to affirm the values that go along with our cause, and provide a reasoned argument for people to buy into them by offering their financial or practical support. Information on progress can also be imparted and special promotional events arranged to raise the profile of the cause through skilful well-targeted advertising.

A big element of selling is the sales pitch, where persuasive argument is used to entice the customers into parting with their money for a particular product. Having been convinced, they thus reject the competition and make a positive choice. In ancient times, rhetoric was a highly valued skill, taught in schools, and exercised in the earliest democracies both in ancient Greece and later in Rome. It no longer has such a prominent place in our education system, although it still has a definite role in political life today. It is interesting how many of our politicians belonged to the debating societies during their time at university, and how many of them cut their teeth speaking in public in the cut and thrust of undergraduate debate. Whether or not our politicians are seen as good advocates of the usefulness of a training in rhetoric is another matter!

There are two ways to view the use of persuasive argument to sell: it can be seen as helpful in that it explores all the reasons to make a certain choice in some depth, and therefore can be seen to be revealing the truth, or it can be seen as a deceptive smokescreen to gain influence over us and persuade us to part with our money for non-essentials. How we perceive it in specific instances is probably affected by our own presuppositions on the subject concerned, and the degree of trust we already have in the protagonists in the debate.

135

Creating an image

In our world today there are many many people, backed by multi-millions of pounds, out to influence our behaviour and unlock our wallets so that we buy their products. Sometimes it seems that the world of advertising has the attitude that people are just there to be manipulated. Yes, there is a healthy scepticism among the population towards advertising, but the fact remains that the major companies obviously feel it is worth it and that they get a good return for all the energy and money invested, or they wouldn't do it. Talk in advertising circles is of creating a brand image, and of using all the tricks of the trade to maintain and strengthen that image.

In fact, a great deal of subtle research is going on all the time to try to bypass our rational minds and influence our behaviour at a deeper level. A key area of research is how to get people to associate a product with warm positive feelings, for the existence of such feelings may be the only thing that differentiates one type of breakfast cereal or margarine from any of its competitors when it comes to hard choices made by shoppers in the supermarket. Advertisers want to control the associations that spring to our minds when their product is mentioned, and to ensure that their product has the most favourable image. Enormous resources are poured into campaigns promoting various products with this aim in mind, backed up by the whole range of modern media.

Packaging versus substance

Market research can help any selling operation be directed to the most lucrative sections of the market, and can ensure that any advertising campaign has maximum effect. It can find out which sections of society are likely to respond to certain products, how they perceive them at present, and what areas need further attention to establish the brand image. Advertising campaigns can then be adapted to take into account how the corporate clients wish their products to be seen, and what the public are likely to respond positively to. This is by no means an easy task, as respondents to market research surveys don't always mean what they say!

Negative aspects of this process include the inevitable need to make judgements about people from external criteria alone, and to pigeon-hole them. There is usually a concentration on those with the greatest capacity to give in order to maximize income. Sometimes facts that customers really ought to know in order to come to a sensible decision may be obscured by clever advertising. These side-effects may not sit easily with a sensitive Christian conscience, especially as the needs of those in the lower socio-economic groups may be ignored and judged to be of little value.

Giving the donors what we think they need

There is also a danger of a certain kind of paternalism drifting into our approach. If we become too concerned about the image we are presenting to the outside world, we will spend increasing time adapting it to the supposed audience, a little like the editor of a TV programme who knows that the appeal of his programme is limited to a certain sector of society. This tendency should give pause for thought – should we assume we are in a position to judge what the recipients of our promotional material need to know? Could we actually be obscuring the truth for the sake of success, and denying the target audience the possibility of a fuller understanding and a more genuine response to the need? Do we actually know best anyway, or should people have every opportunity to make their minds up for themselves?

One approach to marketing ...

* Christ is the image of the invisible God. The Church is itself an image, an icon, almost a sacrament, of God to the world and should behave accordingly.

* Even the packaging matters; everything we engage in must reflect the gospel.

* Marketing techniques need careful analysis before we trust them.

* People should always be treated as made in the image of God and not manipulated.

Another approach to marketing ...

* It is acceptable to adopt any image that does not clearly oppose gospel values.

* Packaging is a peripheral issue.

* It is appropriate to use all the modern marketing methods available to maximize income.

* It's OK to use insights from modern psychology to stimulate giving.

A key Bible principle: Truth

Our faith is worth nothing to us if it is not based on truth. And we have nothing of lasting value to offer a world which is completely free to accept or reject Christianity if we do not pursue truth at every opportunity and adopt it as our standard, our touchstone and the very oxygen we breathe. When considering just how the images we create in the course of our work fit into this approach to life, perhaps we can learn from the incarnation. God is in the communication business too, and seeks to impart knowledge of himself to us through his Son, the image of the invisible God.

Jesus is divinity and Godhead expressed in terms we can understand and with which we can identify, deity distilled down into a single human life. I read long ago the analogy of a large orchestra playing a grand symphony, drawing on the full range of instruments in a panoply of mutually complementary sound, too rich for the human mind to single out individual instruments or the contributions of the various sections. The incarnation was explained as a solo instrument following the same musical theme, with single notes playing out the melody with exquisite beauty and clarity that all could instantly appreciate.

Translating this to the fundraising context, truth is the standard by which we should judge all our work. Of course, every action cannot reflect the whole truth and nothing but the truth, truth in its entirety. But if the way we market and package our fundraising, and indeed the product itself, is not 'true' we are guilty of bringing the gospel we represent into serious disrepute. At the same time we are being dishonest, and risk spiritual damage to ourselves. We must hold every action and the whole operation up to the light and seek transparent truth and honesty at every stage along the way.

Practical issues for discussion

* Someone walks into the church offering a large gift, saying God has told them to hand it over in response to your appeal. You suspect they may be vulnerable, possibly mentally ill. What do you do?

* A guest at a wedding taken in your church who is a partner in a marketing firm offers to help market your campaign for free. The intentions are palpably genuine. Should you accept unconditionally? If not, what areas should be explored first?

* Is it acceptable to use emotive language and vivid photographs in your supporting literature, and what criteria do you use in judging acceptability?

* Is it ethical to change the image you promote according to who you are approaching, highlighting different aspects according to their known sympathies?

20 Clean money, dirty money

Where does the money come from?

Christians will rightly be concerned that any money they raise should come from ethically sound sources, untainted by dubious means used to amass the wealth in the first place. Scruples may be felt about receiving donations from businesses trading in certain areas or from individuals whose lifestyle appears to fall short of some of what may commonly be understood to be God's standards. In some strands of Christianity, there is a deep-rooted suspicion of all involved in commerce, often increasing in direct proportion to the size of the company concerned and its profit margins. Big business is seen as an arena of compromise, with grey areas and grubby overtones.

Certainly at first sight the corporate world of big business can seem far removed from the life of an itinerant Galilean preacher in the first century AD. However, Christians involved in the corporate sector will often vigorously defend the world in which they move and work. They argue that profit is legitimate and leads to the long-term security of their business enterprise, which in turn promotes economic security and widespread prosperity. It provides a justifiable return for investment, and allows companies to continue to offer a service to the public. They draw on a wide range of biblical doctrines to support their position, arguing that they are serving the world, and that as long as their profit is not disproportionate, their staff are fairly paid and safe, and society and the environment are not harmed by their product, they are acting legitimately within the will of God. Indeed in some measure they share his work of creation and preservation of the world.

Grey areas in the corporate world

Christians will nevertheless want to look carefully at the activities and record of particular companies or individuals before deciding whether

140

it would be appropriate to accept money from them, or indeed to make proactive fundraising approaches. There may be a number of shades of grey to be discerned. It is easy to rule out approaches to any firm whose legality is in question. Others may operate within the letter of the law but on closer examination may be seen to be violating its spirit. Still more may be perfectly legal but not follow good practice in terms of policies adopted inside and outside the company. Some may be trading in commodities that could be interpreted as morally dubious; ironically these companies can be the most generous to charitable causes as they seek to improve their profile! Others may be unpopular locally for their employment practices or their effect on the environment.

In passing, it should be remembered that charitable trusts may also be disbursing funds that originally came from areas of activity that might concern some Christians. The same is true of some individuals' personal fortunes. Many trusts have been established using the profits from successful business ventures. Some were established in Victorian times from the fruits of mass labour in adverse working conditions in circumstances that from our twentieth-century perspective appear to represent rank exploitation. Does the passage of time alter the fact that the money was originally derived from such circumstances? Similarly, most trusts continue to draw significant revenue from a portfolio of stocks and shares; have ethical criteria or a drive for maximum profit been used when these portfolios have been put together?

Gambling

Another significant source of funding for many organizations in the charitable sector is derived from different kinds of gambling activity – which range from raffles at parish jumble sales to the National Lottery, with many stops in between. A significant section of the wider Church looks askance at some forms of gambling, while appearing to condone or even actively encourage others. The closer we look the greyer some of the issues become. Definitions become more elusive the harder we try to pin them down – gambling involves an element of risk, but so does taking out an insurance policy. In looking after our own financial resources there may be a blurred line between investment and speculation. Buying a raffle ticket seems a world away from breaking the bank at Monte Carlo.

Many Christians have had a negative attitude to gambling on a number of grounds: that it can lead to compulsive addictive behaviour in certain individuals, that it can bring great hurt and harm to those close to them, that it is immoral as it seeks something for nothing, thus attempting to throw off the natural laws by which our world is governed, and that it often involves a desire for flight from reality and responsibility. Others will recognize with compassion that involvement in some types of gambling brings a little excitement into dull routine lives that so many people have to live, and that activities like the weekly bingo are a much-needed antidote to loneliness and isolation. There's no doubt too that as a fundraising tool they can be extremely effective – even before the advent of lotteries large and small in the 1990s, many charities depended a great deal on raffles, and in some Christian circles they are seen as harmless and a totally legitimate fun way to raise funds.

The National Lottery

The first televised draw for the National Lottery took place in November 1994, and since then the now twice-weekly event has become woven into the national fabric, with many millions glued to their television sets on Wednesday and Saturday evenings, watching coloured balls spinning and rolling, and waiting to see if by any faint (fourteen million to one?) chance they will hit the jackpot. At the time of writing the jury is still out in many circles as to whether the National Lottery is a good or bad thing, whether it is helping or hindering the voluntary sector in Britain and whether vulnerable members of society are contributing to its coffers without seeing a fair proportion of the benefits.

However, there is absolutely no doubt that in a very short space of time the National Lottery has changed the face of grant-making in Britain. The size of the potential sums on offer means that unless a church or charity has serious ethical reservations about applying, any fundraiser working for them would be guilty of serious dereliction of duty not to look into applying. On the other hand it is true to say that the application procedure is arduous and gruelling, and not for the fainthearted. The competition is intense, especially among applications to the National Lottery Charities Board, and many good projects fall by the wayside, sometimes frustratingly for apparent reasons of presentation rather than substance.

Investments

As well as looking at the issue of whether the money we are raising has come from ethically clean sources, many churches and Christian charities would do well to consider where they place their own money once they have got it. Every church has a bank account, and some will amass quite a significant turnover, and take the prudent step of building up some reserves for contingencies, perhaps to the tune of a few months' operating costs.

There have been several significant advances in the viability and availability of ethical investment options in recent years. These initiatives have often been spearheaded by Christians, and this whole area of discussion has then tended to filter out through the charitable sector generally. While charities obviously have a moral duty to invest wisely, much more information is now available to help them identify where to do this. An organization called the Ethical Investment Research Service was set up in 1983 to research the attitudes and behaviour of major companies, using ethical criteria. The Central Finance Board of the Methodist Church and the Central Board of Finance of the Church of England both undertake ethical investments on behalf of churches and charities, achieving respectable rates of return.

Shared Interest is a more recent venture. The concept is simple: individuals can invest sums from £100 to £20,000, which are placed ethically by Shared Interest *en masse* to attract a higher rate of interest than small amounts together would achieve. The difference is shared between the investor and approved charitable projects, usually in the developing world. The individual receives a moderate return, and also has the satisfaction of knowing that they are making a small gesture to redress the overwhelming balance against developing countries in world finance.

One approach to sources of funding...

* All sources of money we accept must be ethically pure.

* God will make it up to us if we decline to pursue certain sources of funding.

* It is morally wrong not to bear in mind how the money was produced in the first place.

* Money raised through gambling or games of chance is unacceptable.

Another approach to sources of funding ...

* The use we put money to is more important than where it came from.

* If we don't accept money from certain sources, others will, and may not use it for such good purposes.

* Money in itself is neutral; we should see a desire to give it by any donor as evidence of God at work.

* It is morally wrong for charities to refuse any legal source of funds.

A key Bible principle: Justice

From the earliest revelations of his nature to the first Hebrews, God revealed himself as having an unswerving commitment to justice, not only for his own people but for all, embracing the strangers, travellers and sojourners whom his people might meet in their wanderings. Into a prehistoric world of wandering ancient near-eastern nomads, when the majority of humanity elsewhere on the planet was still struggling out of the stone age, was born a moral code which has remained the basis of much of the world's thinking on society, ethics and the law ever since. The sophistication of the codes laid down in Leviticus and other parts of the Pentateuch, especially when viewed in their true historical context and taking generations of oral tradition into account, is absolutely breathtaking.

This teaching is reinforced time and time again elsewhere in the Bible, most notably in the Old Testament prophets and the teaching and ministry of Jesus himself. Again and again those who oppress and exploit are condemned. At a time when Judaism had become ever more tied up with interpretations of the letter of the law, Jesus cut through centuries of rabbinical accretions to emphasize that outward behaviour is not God's only concern. Attitudes of the heart are just as important.

Can we therefore dare to ignore issues of justice when approaching financial issues? Our attitude to money and the purposes to which we wish to put it will reveal much about our attitude to justice. Reflection on God's righteousness and holiness as we approach our work is a sensible preparation for involvement in the world of commerce, and will forearm us to make decisions that accord with his justice. By identifying ourselves with God's standards in this way we may even be privileged to bring a prophetic ministry to the modern world, joining with prophets through the ages who have brought God's word to their own generations.

Practical issues for discussion

* What sources of funding would you consider as wrong? Why?

* Is there a difference between proactively seeking money from morally dubious sources and reactively accepting unsolicited donations from them?

* How would you approach debates in the Church about what constitutes an ethically sound source of funding?

* A local company has aroused considerable bad publicity because of repeated pollution episodes. It offers a generous donation to your campaign in return for press coverage. Do you accept?

* An accountant member of the fundraising committee suggests switching funds from an ethical trust fund to maximize profit. What is your response?

21 The root of all evil?

Money: good or bad?

Before money was invented, trade was based on a barter system, and the value of different products was relatively easy to define, indeed often being self-evident. Money represented an attempt on a much wider scale to reduce all aspects of life to quantifiable units, to which a constant value could be assigned. At first, coins needed to be made of precious metals roughly worth the sum they signified; in later times their representative value became sufficient, and the use of paper money grew. We no longer need to hoard our private cache of gold; many transactions now take place electronically without a single coin or note changing hands. The use of credit has mushroomed in the last couple of decades. Most of us use cheque books, most of us have credit cards. The majority of the population are deeply in debt to the banks, having taken out mortgages to secure the roofs over their heads. There is currently a growing awareness of the need to make adequate pension provision for the future. Like it or not, we are locked into a worldwide financial system of credit, and the majority of us are utterly dependent on it.

Money buys security, and can even be said to buy a measure of physical salvation; it is interesting that our financial 'savings' and the religious term 'salvation' come from the same root word. Money saves us from the possibility of future disaster and cushions us from material hardship in the present. It buys power; power to make decisions about our lives, our lifestyle, our future, together with power over others who may be less financially secure than ourselves. The more money we amass, the more opportunities there are to use it to generate further income. The less we have, the fewer options for survival are open to us.

Whether or not Christians like the world of money and its reduction of everything to its own level, if we are to move in the world and be involved in it, we must accept these terms. We may believe that seeing the world from a monetary perspective alone is incomplete and partial, and that there is so much more to life in all its fullness. So many spiritual qualities are impossible to quantify or to put a price on. But we will not be able to change anything from outside; we must address these inadequacies from within.

Corruption

As many Christians will know, the biblical quotation from the New Testament does not assert that money is the root of all evil, but rather that the love of money is the root of all evil. Christians will be particularly aware of the myriad subtle ways in which money can corrupt societies and individuals. Money implies power; as the famous quotation has it, 'power tends to corrupt, and absolute power tends to corrupt absolutely'. We live in an advanced industrial society where money unlocks the doors to further wealth and influence, and materialism is rife. Individual headline-making cases of corruption in high places are the public tip of a very large iceberg.

Motivation

What relevance does this have to the world of fundraising, in a Christian context? I suggest there are several areas which should give us pause for thought. One such area might lie in a closer examination of the motives that lead people to give, and the degree of manipulation of these that a fundraiser may use, consciously or unconsciously. People can give for many reasons, some obvious, some deeply subtle, some entirely honourable and some deeply suspect. Donations can be prompted by thankfulness, obedience to religious dictates, personal involvement in the cause, memory of loved ones, or pure altruism. They can also be prompted by pride, guilt or a desire to impress others; they may be part of a mutually beneficial old-boy network, for commercial gain through accompanying publicity, or a smokescreen to divert attention away from more nefarious activities. A fundraiser often develops an instinct as to what is going on below the surface. Christian fundraisers will want to respond sensitively and appropriately to bring the grace of God into situations where it is needed. They will also want to be sure that they are approaching donors ethically themselves, with no sense of applying undue pressure or manipulation,

147

and no condoning of sin. Where lines are drawn in a sinful imperfect world is for the individual, and/or the institution he or she represents, to define, but awareness that the world is full of shades of grey is a realistic start.

Flattery

It is a sensible use of time for fundraisers to meet with potential donors and those who are in a position to further the cause, to get to know them and what fires their enthusiasm, to build a strong relationship with them, to ensure that they know everything they need to know about your church or organization and the plans you are seeking to bring to fruition. It is right to thank people for their generosity, often not just once but many times. However, just occasionally a tension may arise, as sensitive egos need cosseting and those used to moving in the corridors of power demand a certain deference.

Again, how much time and money should be used in social contacts to promote good relationships with those with power to help? Where does a little modest entertaining of potential supporters in order to promote your cause verge towards bribery? The Christian fundraiser should guard against the undue use of flattery in his armoury of fundraising tools. Any sense of compromise of personal integrity in relationships with those who have the potential to give major gifts indicates that you are on insecure ground. Truth, with tact, should remain the firm foundation on which we stand.

Becoming finance-driven

Sometimes the possibility of substantial sums may be trailed temptingly before hard-pressed fundraisers, but with strings attached. These strings should be very carefully examined, and if they prove problematical it really is better to back off, rather than commit your organization to a course that is out of harmony with the rest of your activities or operations. Sometimes it is not so much strings as the whole direction of a project, which may be substantially unbalanced or radically changed by the possibility of big money. It may sometimes be right to change direction in mid-stream, but this is rare. Hard though it may be to turn your back on large sums with impressive numbers of noughts, money alone is not enough to justify changing the vision. We should never become purely finance-driven in our choices.

Spiritual dangers

The key to our attitude to money should be to keep it in its place. Let it get out of context and it can harden us, distort our perceptions and, when it is proving hard to come by, plunge us into the depths of depression. The power that comes through money and perceived success can itself be a source of corruption. Christian fundraisers need to both pursue success and critique it, being vigilant and periodically examining their own motivations and responses to their successes and failures, possibly with the help of a trusted Christian friend or counsellor. We won't always get it right – after all, we are only human – but errors can be corrected, sins forgiven and a new start made in every circumstance. If it is any encouragement, remaining true to the original ideals will at least ensure that fundraisers remain close to the heart of the institution they are serving, and in close touch with the immediate beneficiaries of their activities.

Baptizing money

Some will seek to argue that it is impossible for us to ensure that all money that may come our way is 'pure', coming from sources that would be regarded as 'clean' by all Christians. However, far from drawing the corollary that money should therefore be refused from many sources and that we should be as choosy as possible, they draw on one of the key Christian doctrines to suggest that all income should be embraced. Redemption is at the heart of the gospel. Is it not possible that by taking money which may have originated from dubious sources and putting it to holy uses, we are in fact redeeming it, transforming darkness to light? This argument can be made more compelling when it is pointed out that if Christians are too proud to accept such funds, there are plenty of others with fewer scruples who will eagerly grasp at it, and use it for purposes which are far less pleasing to God. Such pragmatism echoes the approach of the Church many times through history when encountering pagan patterns of life. Often these were not so much destroyed as 'baptized', and absorbed with distinctive new overtones into the service of the Church.

One approach to money ...

* Money is a necessary evil in a basically sinful world.

* We should shun temptation and danger of corruption, and remain unworldly.

149

* Spiritual purity transcends all worldly matters in importance.

* The Kingdom is to come; the need for money will be superseded.

Another approach to money ...

* We are called to full involvement in the world, including money.

* The Church's mission is to transform the world, including the financial world.

* Dirty hands are inevitable as we follow Jesus' example and get involved.

* Money can to some extent buy justice and further the kingdom of God.

* Even money from dubious sources can be redeemed by the uses we put it to.

A key Bible principle: Love

If asked to express the essence of the Christian faith in one word, the majority of Christians would probably answer 'love'. The lyrical hymn to love, which we know as 1 Corinthians 13, says it all. Faith, hope and love abide, but the greatest of them all is love.

Christian love though is no saccharine-sweet response to the world we live in, with all its hurts and imperfections. It is realistic, tough and costly. It involves every level of our being; the rational and the will as well as the emotions. St Augustine may have advocated that Christians love God and do what they like; but of course the fact is that what we actually like to do changes radically when our love begins to approximate more closely to the Christian ideal – which is precisely his point.

Love seeks the good of others, and puts the common good above that of the selfish individual. It is altruism in action. It was perfectly embodied for all time in the life, death and resurrection of Jesus, and has been enshrined in Scripture for our instruction and edification. It can grow cold and die, but if cherished and tended it can burn brightly and shine through all we do. It can be brought to bear on every situation we face, challenging our deepest motivation, our world-view, our priorities, the place of our small contribution to the Kingdom in the wider perspective. If love is first in our hearts, we may make mistakes, we may experience failures, but our work will not be in vain, and we ourselves will remain intact in our Christian service.

Practical issues for discussion

* What safeguards can be introduced to make sure money does not become all-important?

* What checks and balances should be in place to avoid temptation and corruption?

* When does tact become flattery when dealing with the rich and influential?

* If you were offered £100,000 but acceptance involved handing over ultimate control of your project, would you accept?

22 Ends and means

Do the ends we use ever justify the means? If so, which means are permissible and which are beyond the pale? This question has exercised the minds of moral theologians for centuries, so a quick and easy answer distilled into a couple of lines is hardly likely to appear on the pages of this book! However, traditional church teaching has established a few guidelines to help us make moral choices in all areas of life – including our professional and business lives – which may have something to say to some of the ethical questions that arise in fundraising.

Is success all-important?
Most Christians will accept that wealth-generation is a perfectly legitimate aim to have in our working lives, and that it is a prerequisite for a modern civilized society. Success in business dealings is one outward measure of how much society is benefiting from our work. However, success can easily become an all-consuming end in itself, in the same way that we know that a disproportionate grasping after money can distort our lives. If it does become an end in itself, more highly valued than the needs of the society it serves, corruption so often follows. Success, often hand in hand with increased profit, leads to greater power, but for the Christian this will imply greater responsibility. 'Much is required of those to whom much is given.' There is a paradox here; the Christian will want to both promote success, and also submit it to analysis and judgement in the light of Scripture.

The danger of idolatry
When pursuit of profit and success becomes an end in itself, it effectively becomes a form of idolatry, set up in the place of God, even worshipped in his place. Increasingly our time, energy, minds and wills will be sacrificed at its altar. Instead of being carefully hedged about with

checks and balances to keep it in proportion, successful fundraising can become a monstrous machine of wheels and cogs, running for its own sake rather than driven by genuine needs. It demands ever-increasing commitment and effort; the targets set rise inexorably whether or not the original vision for the cause has been achieved or transcended. Anyone who challenges this idolatry runs the risk of being perceived to be an enemy to the all-powerful idol that has been created, and of being scapegoated.

Should we fundraise at all?

Some Christians may think that any fundraising at all is a totally inappropriate activity for Christians working for a Christian cause. Prayer yes, fasting yes, sacrificial personal giving yes, but entering the market place and soliciting support emphatically no. If it is the Lord's will that a project happen, the money will come in regardless. The Christian has no need to use subtle modern techniques hijacked from the business world. It is interesting that many personnel with responsibility for raising funds in a Christian context (for example those with responsibility for this area at a diocesan level in the Church of England) will be described as stewardship advisers first and foremost rather than fundraisers. The term 'stewardship' is usually defined as encompassing the development of the whole range of gifts and talents the Christian can lay at the service of the wider Church, and not just the giving of money.

This is an interesting issue, and deserves a thoughtful response. Useful related areas of debate include the activity of God in the secular world – if God chooses to be involved in the whole range of human activity, should we limit the methods used in his service to generate income? Are we too eager to distinguish between what is clean and unclean, just as the early Jewish Christians had to learn not to be bound by the Law? Can we be salt and light and a witness to Christ in the very act of fundraising as we reach out to all the various sources of available funds?

Is it right to fundraise for ourselves?

Some will look at the deeper needs of humanity in our time and ask how any caring person can ignore these to devote time to more parochial, even selfish needs and concerns. Others may see issues on a global scale dwarfing all other concerns; ecological matters and concern for the future of the planet can eclipse national or local causes. We are so well off in the so-called First World; how can we seek more riches and benefits for ourselves in the face of the utter deprivation that is so widespread in other parts of the world? We are all so rich in material terms – surely the gospel implies an ethical imperative that we sell all we have and give it to the poor.

It is certainly right and good to have our horizons widened and to seek to look at our world from a divine perspective. It is all too easy to concentrate on our own needs selfishly and forget the plight of millions who remain out of sight and out of mind, apart from brief soundbites on news bulletins that may tweak a heartstring for a second or two before being swamped by other images. However, it is also true that we are called to 'bloom where we are planted', and to work diligently in the particular context in which we are set. Working as I do in an institution of higher education may not at first sight seem to be at the cutting-edge of radical change to create a better world. To some (not necessarily those who have experienced it from the inside!) it may appear to be a bastion of privilege.

But then again, I consider all the lives of gifted energetic and idealistic young people who have passed through these doors through the decades, who spend several of their most formative years on the threshold of adulthood here. This environment seeks to equip them for a lifetime of work and service, at a far deeper level than the purely intellectual and academic. Perhaps the influence of education for good is far more extensive and effective than appears at first sight. None of us will know the true extent of the influence and value of our work this side of the grave. But if God has indeed got a plan for his world and holds it in his hands, our primary concern should be to be obedient in serving him in our own small corner. God is big enough to take responsibility for the rest.

Perhaps a suitable balance when fundraising for ourselves is to look for an external project with a much broader application to support in tandem with our own needs. This stops us from becoming insular or selfish and keeps us sensitive to the needs of others. It fosters a sense of common purpose and mission with those in various kinds of needs in contexts very different from our own. Those who are involved in partnerships like this will very often find to their surprise that the benefit is not all one way, and that there is much to receive and learn through such contact.

Should we seek money beyond the Church?

One particular example of the balance between ends and means is seen in the tension in some Christian circles over the issue of whether it is right for Christians to fundraise outside the Church for Christian causes. Some will take a kind of pride in maintaining a purity of approach which says that God's people pay for all work in his name. Others may acknowledge God at work in the wider world and wish to extend the boundaries, with an attitude that bears some resemblance to that of the apostle Peter after his vision in Joppa (Acts 10), when it dawned on him finally that the gospel extended to the gentile world and was not confined within the Jewish community. As with so many ethical issues, perhaps each organization should think through their own position, bearing in mind always God's tendency to transcend our structures and burst through the boundaries we may impose.

Christian ethics

It goes without saying that the Christian seeks to do God's will and be obedient to his laws in everything. However, life does not consist of simple black and white choices and when the issues include shades of grey, the law of 'double effect' has often been applied by Christian ethicists. This allows that an action may be undertaken even if this means that an evil may also occur as an unavoidable side-effect. Over the centuries various qualifications have been added to help us discern practical examples of good and evil. Thus such an action may only be followed under certain conditions. One distinguished writer on the subject has summarized these conditions as follows:

> In the 19th century, actions involving certain evils were said to be justifiable under a four-fold condition: (1) The action from which evil results is good or indifferent in itself; it is not morally evil. (2) The intention of the agent is upright – i.e., the evil effect is sincerely not intended. (3) The evil effect must be equally immediate causally with the good effect, for otherwise it would be a means to the good effect and would be intended. (4) There must be a proportionately grave reason for allowing the evil to occur. (R. A. McCormick, SJ, in *A New Dictionary of Christian Ethics*, ed. J. Macquarrie and J. Childress, SCM Press, 1986, pp. 162–3.)

Another approach takes as a starting-point Jesus' teaching about the centrality of love. Most Christians believe that love is the key to Christian behaviour. This has led to a distinct strand of ethical thinking, first consciously developed as 'situation ethics' by John Stuart Mill in the nineteenth century. In situation ethics, actions are examined and judged according to how they match up to love, inevitably involving an element of subjectivity. Rules and moral laws are there to advise, but they should be our slaves and not our masters, and do not have the power of absolute veto over us. The early proponents of situation ethics felt that it was possible to compare and contrast the outcome of various actions and to identify the most loving way forward, using various factors on a scale or calculus to make judgements. However, measuring and comparing love has proved to be rather more difficult than they initially supposed. Once we abandon certain absolutes, the waters can get very muddy indeed.

A third approach rooted in Scripture and often resorted to by Christians with moral choices to make develops the train of thought laid out in 1 Corinthians 8. This deals with the New Testament issue of consumption of food that has first been offered to idols. St Paul's primary concern here is not whether or not food offered to idols is demonized or whether the idols themselves reflect the existence of pagan deities, but to insist that Christian liberty is not exploited at the expense of weaker brethren whose consciences may be disturbed by such practices. Put into a modern fundraising context, the underlying principle behind this passage implies that whereas some in the church might be quite happy about seeking or receiving funds from a whole range of sources, if this upsets or offends others in the church their concerns should be listened to and taken seriously. This may even mean moulding the fundraising policy of the whole church to take their sensitivities into account. This is not because of the intrinsic rights or wrongs of such fundraising sources *per se*, but because people are always more important than money, and it is clearly a sin to act in a way which injures the conscience and therefore damages the faith of other members of the church. Of course, faith is then needed in even greater measure that God will bless and honour such an approach.

One approach to ends and means ...

* There are moral absolutes; the Ten Commandments never change.

* It is absolutely wrong to let the ends justify the means.

* Some means should never be used.

* God's word is clear and binding for all time.

Another approach to ends and means ...

* There are no absolutes, just guidelines.

* New situations require new interpretations of eternal truths.

* All means are acceptable if used with loving intent.

* Money raised by any means buys the power to make transformations for good.

A key Bible principle: Faith

Faith is, according to the writer of the epistle to the Hebrews, the assurance of things hoped for, the conviction of things not seen. Possessing it alters the whole context of our lives. This world is no longer all there is, or all that matters. There is a wider canvas to our lives, an extra dimension beyond space and time and the physical universe. If Christ was not raised from the dead, Christians are of all people most to be pitied, for they dance to a different tune which is not of this world.

Relative rights and wrongs are suddenly subject to absolute standards as revealed by God when faith becomes a factor for us. Truth and justice, love and faith each have their impact on the decisions we make and the way we conduct our personal and professional lives. Faith particularly impacts upon us as we depart from the ways of the world, and consciously disregard the wisdom it offers. Turning down money or refusing to use certain channels when pursuing it may look like pure folly to the world. It may only be with the eyes of faith that we can see a justification for acting as we do, and can rest with easy consciences, knowing that when the whole picture is complete we shall be vindicated. God is in control, and there are many biblical promises to hold on to and claim for our own that will nourish us and nerve us for the fight.

157

Practical issues for discussion

* What qualities are most important in a Christian fundraiser?

* What fundraising activities are inappropriate for Christians?

* Is it acceptable to use your friends and family to secure further fundraising contacts?

* Would you consider selling a valuable possession of the church (a painting, silverware, etc.) to release funds for your project?

* Another church or charity is pursuing a similar aim to your own. You believe your project is stronger than theirs. How do you react?

* Another church or charity is pursuing a similar aim to your own. You believe your project is weaker than theirs. How do you react?

---

23 Lessons from modern fundraising for the Church

The longer I have been involved in fundraising, the more I am convinced of the many parallels between fundraising and the gospel. Both are concerned with winning people to a new point of view, adjusting their priorities, and seeking allegiance not just from their wallets, but to a very real degree from their hearts and minds. There are particular parallels with evangelism. Fundraisers seek to win donations and gifts, often in a carefully orchestrated and thoughtfully planned way, just as evangelists and missionaries periodically carry out special campaigns to win converts. Modern fundraising may have important lessons to teach the Church, with applications which extend beyond its income-generating activities.

A professional approach

In the last twenty years the fundraising profession has mushroomed in number and in influence in the charity world. Whereas at one time only the big-name charities employed specialist professional fundraisers, often working singly and occasionally in small teams, now the vast majority of charities employ highly trained and experienced personnel, sometimes in sizeable teams. Regional fundraisers are often appointed to complement the work in the charity's headquarters. Universities, colleges and schools increasingly employ professionals, as do hospital trusts, hospices, theatres, arts groups, sports organizations and many others. At the same time as the number of jobs has exploded, the expectations of professional standards of work have grown. At one time retired captains of industry or those who had held high rank in the armed services found a little gentle fundraising to be a suitable occupation for their final working years, allowing them to exploit to some extent a certain old-boy network among those of similar age, outlook and background on the boards of companies and trusts. Those days are

159

fading fast. Fundraising is an attractive profession for many of our brightest young graduates as they move into the world of employment with high ideals and the desire to make a difference for good in the world. The ethos in which they work owes more to the modern world of public relations than gentlemen's clubs. It may not be overstating the case to assert that in some areas the Church needs to make the same kind of transition.

Standards, training, accreditation

Some years ago the need was recognized for a professional institute to guard standards and promote best practice among fundraisers, to lobby on behalf of charities on relevant issues and to provide a network of support. The Institute of Charity Fundraising Managers (ICFM) has grown into a major force in fundraising in Britain today, listened to by government on issues concerning the voluntary sector and providing a network of regional groups run by fundraisers for fundraisers, served by a small staff and office headquarters in London. It produces a regular national newsletter, and occasional papers on topical subjects, including codes of practice on particular aspects of fundraising.

In its earlier years it aspired to be a major provider of accredited training for fundraisers, available to its members at foundation and higher levels. This served to assure potential employers that key areas of competence had been achieved and a measure of experience and knowledge could be assumed in applicants who had passed through the levels. Their vision has now expanded to cover the giving of accreditation based on prior experience, for fundraisers who have been doing effective work for some years without having necessarily attended the right course to produce a corresponding paper qualification. They also validate some of the training providers who have sprung up around the country, providing seminars and courses on every conceivable aspect of the fundraiser's role.

It could be argued that there needs to be much more promoting of in-service training among the clergy in order to increase their effectiveness and maximize the skills and abilities they bring to their roles. There are hopeful signs in many Anglican dioceses that this issue is being addressed, with increased opportunities for continuing ministerial education in the Church. However, the initiative seems to lie with individual clergy and ministers in following up the opportunities that are available. A slightly more proactive approach might yield even further fruit. For many clergy in isolated situations there are tremendous benefits to be gained from such training, where lessons successful elsewhere in the country can be adapted to their context, kindling new enthusiasm and hope in their ministries. Of course, the clergy are not the only ones with a role to fulfil for the Church. It could indeed be argued that training opportunities are also of paramount importance for the laity, to enable the whole body of the Church to function to its full potential.

Strategic approach

Over the past couple of decades many major charities have realized that they need to think through the most basic of issues about their reason for existence and purpose. Sometimes it would be healthy for church organizations to go through the same process. What are they actually there to do in practical terms, and how should they go about achieving it? It may no longer be enough to assume that they are fulfilling a valid role merely because they exist.

Having a properly considered and structured strategy can help both churches and charities become much more proactive, instead of waiting for people to beat a path to their door when the fancy takes them. This is actually very similar to the way Jesus worked. His ministry was not confined within the synagogue, but was a wandering one, travelling to where the people were, and teaching them in terms they could understand, with content packed full of examples that struck chords with their everyday lives. He identified a small band of followers with great care, who in time became the nucleus of the early Church. Within a few years the gospel was being proclaimed in the very heart of the Roman empire, before the emperor himself.

Evaluation

An openly agreed strategy makes it much easier for all involved to identify a range of indicators for success, to measure outcomes and highlight the various areas of the organization's life which should receive further attention. The evaluation process helps us learn and reflect on what we are doing and on the effectiveness of our methods. Trends in charitable giving these days are closely observed by fundraising professionals across the voluntary sector, league tables are drawn up and statistics are widely analysed to see what insights can be deduced. The Church could learn from this hunger for effectiveness. Too often success and church growth occur in isolated pockets, with little reflection on the factors that may have led to the fanning of a small spark of life into a great flame of vibrant activity. There is comparatively little sharing between deaneries or circuits, and even less between denominations, of what is working. Churches are left in isolation each to learn hard lessons for themselves, sometimes through a painful process of trial and error. In the modern age of instant communication there must be something wrong in this.

Techniques and technology

Charities have shown a willingness to embrace modern technology and to invest in IT and training for staff to exploit the opportunities it offers to the full. The use of databases allows for a wealth of information about supporters to be available at the touch of a button or the click of a mouse. Spreadsheets have taken much of the agony out of full and detailed accounting. More and more charities have Web pages on the Internet, and use email for quick, easy and cheap communication. Prices are coming down all the time, and most churches with the will to be at the forefront of this new technology should be able to at least dabble a toe in the water if they really believe that communication lies near the heart of the gospel.

Concern with ethics

It may seem strange to assert that churches can learn something from the secular charity world when it comes to ethics. However, many charities have taken over principles of good practice in the way the institution operates from the best of the corporate world, and some of these make very good sense indeed, and serve to protect all involved. An example is the proper laying out of accounts, and the establishment of an audit trail of all money coming into and flowing out of the organization.

Another example is the very open and supportive networking that goes on between fundraisers. By and large, people are willing to support and help each other to quite a substantial degree. There is little of the paranoia and secrecy or the cut-throat rivalry that characterizes the worlds of advertising and marketing, although breaches of confidentiality and conflicts of interest are studiously avoided. I have come across numerous examples of those who are highly placed in the fundraising world and who have become national names within the profession, who have been willing to take time and care to advise new-comers. There is a general desire to raise standards and the esteem in which fundraising as a profession is held by the world at large, for the benefit of all. It would be good to sense such a relaxed attitude to 'the competition' among the churches, and more of a sense of pulling together to speak with a common voice for the good of all who stand for Christ.

Flexibility

Meetings of fundraisers are often notable for great openness to others working in the same field who come from very different perspectives. The desire to listen and learn from each other, even when the charities represented lie at the opposite end of the spectrum and might be expected to have if anything a mild antipathy to each other, is impressive. Good fundraisers often excel at lateral thinking, and a throwaway comment from one context is often taken and transformed into a successful fundraising technique, given a slight twist along the way. Flair, opportunism and an adventurous attitude to risk-taking are not far below the surface in some of the most successful fundraising campaigns in recent history for charities – but these are not necessarily the characteristics which first come to mind when we think of the Church. In particular, many successful charities allow a certain flexibility, which enables them to seize the moment and catch the public mood in their work. The Church in contrast, and occasionally undeservedly, is still perceived to be a monolithic backward-looking institution, where a fierce rearguard action is fought over every change, however small.

24 **What the Church can teach the fundraising world**

Growing relationships

Many fundraising gurus talk today in terms of relationship fundraising – encouraging fundraisers to build an ever-closer link with donors, drawing them into a deeper identification with the cause, hustling them along through a theoretical lifetime of giving from a first casual donation to a final bequest after death. Clergy and ministers obviously seek a growing commitment from their flock too, with a gradual drawing into the very heart of the life of the Church and an ever-deepening devotion to Christ. There are many parallels, and many techniques which church leaders have been using for centuries, which the world of fundraising is just catching on to.

Many charities in their fundraising work will concentrate on the relatively small number of potential donors who have the capacity to give major sums to the cause. Churches, however, have traditionally drawn their income from a large number of members (who are already committed to the cause) giving relatively small sums which cumulatively amass a significant total. Most church members who give do so in obedience to biblical teaching and through a strong sense of identification with the life and aims of the Church. Many charities would be absolutely thrilled to have such a highly committed membership list giving so regularly and sacrificially. The personal regular attendance of many of the membership at church worship, where biblical teaching on giving can be imparted through sermons, is obviously a tremendous advantage for churches. This is often reinforced by group teaching on stewardship themes in smaller meetings and house-groups.

Where appropriate, Christian charities as well as churches can tap into the practice many individual Christians follow of setting aside up to a tenth of their income for 'the Lord's work'. Church congregations themselves often follow a similar principle, setting aside a proportion of overall income to be given away to the wider work of the Church. It is not unknown for larger successful churches to give money to poorer struggling congregations as part of this process. Where there is a strong Christian element to the project or campaign for which the Christian fundraiser is working, he or she can certainly learn from the experience of local churches in presenting the cause not just as worthy of occasional generosity but as part of the Christian obligation to give, and in looking for ways to encourage a deep-seated commitment.

Teamwork: the body of Christ

Today's society carries much stress on the individual. However, the Bible has a very different approach to life and work. As Christians we are part of a body that should function as a harmonious unit. Many churches these days are far more conscious of 'every member ministry', with gifts and talents put at the disposal of the whole Church for the common good. Interestingly, parts of industry are beginning to take this approach too, with many companies arranging their workforce into teams who work together on particular assignments, rather than the traditional hierarchy from management to shopfloor. Management courses often involve team-building exercises, and interview procedures often seek to identify employees who have good interpersonal and communication skills who will fit easily into the team approach to work.

In fundraising, the need to work as a team is also extremely important. Even the lone fundraiser in a small organization will need to know how to motivate and engage a wide range of people behind the cause to maximize the effectiveness of their work. Also, the smaller the fundraising professional team the more important it is for the individual worker to feel personally supported by the wider organization. Any gathering of professional fundraisers will throw up a number of plaintive cries from the heart from those who feel misunderstood and undervalued by their superiors and colleagues working in different departments in the charity. Sometimes this extends to those actually involved in delivering the services the charity exists to offer, and even to the beneficiaries who receive those services. Mutual support within 'every member ministry' is a key truth from New Testament times being rediscovered in the Church today, and many charities could do well to adapt such an approach in their own management structures.

165

Christian ethics: a framework for fundraising and for life
The Christian faith has many ethical principles to inform all commercial and business life, which are just as relevant to the world of fundraising. The treating of all people as created in the image of God and therefore imbued with sanctity and to be valued as such is one basic tenet. Anything which dehumanizes society or the individual, or smacks of manipulation, is anathema to such teaching. The absolute need for truth and honesty, and the rooting out of all that involves deceit, whether in the heart or its outworking in action, is another 'given' for the Christian. Lives and work founded on anything less will prove to be built on sand rather than rock. The Ten Commandments provide a structure for behaviour which is largely negative in tone with a list of 'Thou shalt nots', into which the teaching of Jesus breathes the positive 'Thou shalt love the Lord thy God with all thy heart, and with all thy soul, and with all thy strength, and with all thy mind, and thy neighbour as thyself.' This gives an overriding ethical principle to which all our behaviour can be submitted. Love here is taken in its fullest definition to include all the breadth of God's justice and truth.

Prayer
When fundraising in a Christian context, one enormous benefit Christians have over those who work in a secular environment and from a secular perspective is the power of prayer. Whether or not your theology allows you to assume that God knows your situation personally, hears your requests and will answer in simple direct terms, the experience of the Church through all the centuries is that prayer does make a difference. Regular corporate worship in a church or Christian charity can be particularly helpful for those working within it. It stills the heart and nerves the will for further endeavour. It engenders confidence and purpose. It helps the whole team focus on a common aim and draws them closer together as each draws closer to God. It broadens the context in which tasks are considered and takes out some of the strain and stress as responsibility for ultimate success is seen to be so much greater than the work of one fallible individual.

Perseverance
Viewing fundraising work from a Christian perspective as an aspect of service to God reduces stress by absolving the fundraiser from sole personal responsibility for the outcome. But this does not have the effect

of leading the Christian fundraiser to shrug their shoulders when the going gets tough, heave a fatalistic sigh and take things easier for a while until the prospects look a bit brighter. By a strange irony this removal of responsibility actually redoubles personal motivation and determination to offer one's best efforts to God. This can be particularly valuable in times when the going is hard, tangible progress and visible results are being elusive and it is not at all clear where the next donation will arrive from. A whole sea of pressures can combine at times to overwhelm the beleaguered fundraiser; hard questions about cost-effectiveness within the organization, disappointments as hoped-for sums do not materialize, lack of resources to invest in thorough fundraising research, can each sap morale and weaken resolve. An awareness of the presence of God as one who draws us out to safety in times of storm and tempest and sets us back on solid ground is a tremendous asset. Faith that God is in control can stem the rising tide of panic when things look black.

The wider context: there is more to life than fundraising!

It can be good for all of us to hear that we are not the most important cogs in any particular machine. The world will not grind to a shuddering halt if we do not experience perpetual success beyond all expectations of those around us, and similarly we will not have single-handedly changed the whole course of human history if we experience a measure of success beyond our own wildest dreams. Success and failure are both impostors with a disturbing habit of perverting our view of ourselves and our world. A much safer and more satisfactory world-view is one based on Christian values and biblical truth. Fundraisers are in the money business, but we are reminded that there are far more important things around than mere pounds, shillings and pence. Money is actually often seen as a hindrance to the gospel rather than a help, and its acquisition, albeit for charitable purposes, brings with it enormous responsibilities.

We all need to be reminded occasionally that God is interested in each of us individually, not for what we can do or achieve, but for who we are. His love for us is singularly unimpressed by achievements and worldly success, even when carried out directly for the good of the Church and the world he created. His concern is both for the heart, and the whole person. Whatever our task in life, however large or small it is, it should never be allowed to eclipse these truths. Sometimes we need to give ourselves permission to be whole people rather than units of production. It is certainly thoroughly Christian so to do.

A cause worth fighting for

When it comes down to it, for the Christian, faith gives meaning and purpose to human existence. It provides answers (or at least some pretty useful pointers) to basic questions such as who, what, where, why am I, and what am I doing here? If just a little of this sense of purpose and assurance is transferable to Christian fundraisers as they consider their work, they will have a solid foundation upon which to build their endeavours. Motivation will be high but stress will be low. Under God it is their part to labour in obedience to the utmost of their ability, using all available methods that accord with what they know of the nature of God. They will be 100 per cent sure of the validity of their cause and will give 100 per cent effort, but they will know that the burden does not lie upon their shoulders alone. It is shared with One whose shoulders are broader than theirs and whose wisdom and resources are infinite.

PART FOUR   **CASE STUDIES**

25 Case Studies

Case study 1 The organ

The site of the first study is an ancient market town in a northern diocese. The parish has a population of 15,000, socially diverse but mainly in owner-occupier accommodation. There are about 450 on the electoral roll; the main focus of Sunday worship is a morning Parish Communion with about 200 adults and 60 children. The church was originally a collegiate foundation, built between 1200 and 1400, and is regarded as one of the finest Gothic buildings in Europe. Special services are held on the major festivals and for outside organizations. The building is also a regular venue for concerts of varying types.

In the mid-1970s a major fabric restoration appeal was launched, raising £1 million to clean and restore the stonework of the building. At that time the need for considerable expenditure on the organ was already identified. This need was underlined by a further professional report completed in July 1992, indicating that total expenditure in the region of £165,000 was urgently needed. The vicar decided that action on this matter could no longer be deferred. In October 1992 he drafted a confidential document for the PCC outlining the need for action.

No lay person was available to take responsibility for chairing the appeal, so the vicar in effect worked extra hours, taking on this role in addition to existing parish responsibilities. An appeal committee was set up, and a number of patrons invited to link their names to the cause.

The vicar was concerned in his strategy to break down the overall total into manageable units that seemed achievable to all involved. The strategy document identified several different constituencies which might be willing to support the appeal, then proceeded to adapt the fundraising approach to each constituency as appropriate. Thus an appeal for direct giving was made to the congregation, complemented by an appeal to those who attended special services. At the same time those trusts were targeted which might be expected to give because of the importance of the church as a building and of the organ as an instrument of national importance. Local individuals who might sympathize with these aims were also targeted, and the final potential constituency of support was identified as those involved in the musical culture of the area.

Different people on the appeal committee took responsibility for various areas; the vicar himself took on the applications to trusts and other grant-making bodies. Others concentrated on events and concerts. A simple, clear and attractive brochure was produced comparatively cheaply, with a print run of 20,000 costing just 12p each.

A launch occasion was planned once the campaign was seen to be on the move. The existing organ fund contributed £10,000, augmented by a further £10,000 from a legacy, £20,000 from the Friends of X Church and a single £5,000 Gift Aided donation from an individual. This allowed a launch event with substantial progress already made towards the total. The inaugural concert was sponsored by British Gas, with a local orchestra supporting a top violin soloist. The event brought people together, raised the profile of the campaign and raised a further £2,000 in one night, also playing a significant part in several more donations.

The local congregation and those having a personal link with the church raised approximately £20,000 through direct giving, and this was augmented by a further £45,000 from charitable trusts and other grant-making bodies. The vicar handled the applications to trusts personally, and the 250 applications made constituted the most time-consuming aspect of the appeal for him. In contrast, relatively little was raised from local companies and businesses. The town is set in a rural area with few large businesses to call upon, and many companies in the wider area had been cutting back on charitable giving in common with trends across the country since the boom years of the 1980s.

When the campaign was already under way, a chance conversation with the borough council led to the exploration of the possibility of European funding for the appeal. The vicar had been in contact with councillors on other matters, who were then able to suggest the possibility of application to the ERDF structural fund, as the county had been declared a priority area for this. A visit to the relevant EU office led eventually to a formal application for funding on the basis of strengthening the local economy by enhancing the church's appeal as a tourist attraction. The form-filling was detailed and time-consuming, but led to a successful outcome, with the EU agreeing to fund 45 per cent of the total costs. With the other monies already in place as outlined above, this effectively achieved the target just three months after the launch, and well ahead of schedule. The appeal was left open and some more small sums continued to trickle in for some time.

On reflection the vicar would not have approached this project differently in any way, except possibly by building in a more substantial sum for contingencies, as costs rose during the appeal to £180,000. The benefits of the appeal were many; members of the church were pleasantly surprised at how quickly it was achieved.

Case study 2 **Youth worker**

The previous case study from X Church outlined various details about the parish and the life of the church. This second project, to fund the salary for a full-time youth worker for five years, followed on from the successful appeal which had raised £180,000 to restore the organ. It formed part of a natural progression, as the time was now seen to have come to invest more deeply in the actual ministry of the Church as opposed to the fabric of the building.

The church already had a staff of three full-time clergy, a vicar and two curates. There were also six readers, a part-time administrator, and a parish office staffed by one full-time and one part-time secretary. However, despite these comparative riches in terms of staff resources, a serious need to have an effective ministry to the town's young people was identified. In the past, one of the curates was usually delegated to oversee youth work as part of his or her overall brief; but even when the individual concerned had a particular expertise in this field, it could not occupy the majority of their time. The need for a full-time person to take on youth work if the church was to make any significant impact on young people in the town was widely recognized.

Once again, initial discussions took place between the vicar and the PCC, leading to an interim report on 'Youth and Outreach Work'. The need for a full-time professional to take on the work and grapple seriously with the issues involved was clearly identified.

Having discussed this verbally at one PCC meeting, the vicar subse-

172

quently contacted a number of other churches with salaried youth workers on their staff for information, then produced a written document for the PCC arguing for the appointment of a full-time youth worker on a five-year contract basis. The cost of salary, essential expenses and an allowance for inflation was estimated to be £20,000 per annum or £100,000 for the five years.

The vicar suggested that this particular project should be the recipient of the income from the church's next annual gift day, which was held regularly at Harvest Festival. He felt that this post should be financed primarily if not entirely by those within the worshipping community of the church, on pragmatic as well as theological grounds. The town was perceived as being a relatively affluent area, without the extremes of deprivation or social dysfunction which might lever in significant funds from statutory sources or many charitable trusts. Some trusts were approached in the course of the appeal, but no brochure was produced. Instead, a letter was carefully drafted to all members on the electoral roll 'and all who are associated with X Church'. This was sent out prior to the gift day, laying out the context of the project, the aims, a brief description of the work a youth leader should undertake, the benefits which would flow from the appointment and the costs involved.

He was careful to break down the total sum (£100,000) into manageable chunks that those on average incomes might feel able to afford. He suggested that 120 covenants of £10 per month would be enough to raise the total, while recognizing that some might feel able to give more, and some less. The existing covenant secretary was designated to administer this new fund, encouraging covenanted or Gift Aided donations wherever possible.

The letter was accompanied by a simple pledge form allowing parishioners to indicate their intentions. The vicar topped and tailed each letter, sometimes adding a short 'PS' to make the approach as personal as possible. The immediate response was sufficient to indicate that the whole project was viable. Pledges of £40,000 were made on the gift day itself, a figure which rose to £70,000 within a month. This encouraged the church to proceed to an appointment.

Several special services in the course of the year gave money from the collection to the Youth Fund; for example a special service for judges raised nearly £1,000 on the day, and provoked a further single donation of £1,000 from an individual. Once again, targeted trusts were approached, and although no national trusts responded positively, some £4,000 was given by local trusts. At the time of writing, the fund stands at £93,000, twelve months on from the launch.

Possibly because this project was primarily aimed at the existing worshipping community, there have been some positive by-products for the life of the church through the fundraising exercise. To have been involved in two successful fundraising projects in succession drew the congregation together by raising morale, expectations and faith, uniting the parish under the vicar's leadership. Several 'lapsed' electoral roll members were drawn back into the life of the church through the personal approach and the project. In a wider context, the ability to employ an extra member of staff will inevitably deepen the commitment of many younger members, build links with the local community and be instrumental in bringing some to the faith, thus enriching the whole Church.

Case study 3 **Church reordering**

This is the story of a small Anglican church in a northern diocese, set in a farming and residential community. At the beginning of the project, the church building was 75 years old and had no special architectural merit; the electoral roll numbered 37, comprising mainly people aged over fifty. The parish had recently been incorporated into one benefice with a neighbouring parish. It owned a dilapidated church hall, which had been a focus for the community for many years. This hall was now in a dangerous condition.

A new vicar arrived as the church family was facing up to a difficult decision: whether to refurbish this hall or to demolish it and start again. This was extremely difficult for parishioners, who had seen many other facilities closed or demolished in their community in recent years. Many of them had vivid memories of happy occasions in it. However, despite the difficult emotions involved, the new vicar felt on cost grounds that to demolish was the only way forward.

After prayer and consideration, the decision was taken to create new facilities to replace the hall within the existing church building. By partitioning off the north aisle a small room for 20 and a larger room for up to 50 could be created, plus kitchen and toilets and a new lighting system for the whole church.

Having taken this decision, the vicar saw the main immediate priority as being to build the people up in prayer and to reawaken their faith and initiative. He organized a 'Celebration of gifts', to take place on Ascension Day. Many contributed different kinds of crafts for exhibition, and the local council loaned archive material relating to the village's history which was also on show. The church was full all day with visitors, beginning with a morning service and ending with an evening charity auction. Over £1,000 was raised.

The vicar then put it to the congregation that the central core to the project would have to be raised through giving, and that this had to be in place before further fundraising could follow. He refused to look outside the parish for money until a substantial sum was in place. He also stopped all raffles and fundraising based on chance as a matter of principle. His strategy was to get people to aim high, but to approach the overall target in manageable portions within realistic reach.

An architect already connected to the church was engaged, and the overall total needed to do all the work was estimated at £67,000. The architect introduced the parish to a fundraising consultant who gave advice on methods of individual giving. A separate treasurer for the fund was appointed from within the parish. An approach asking for small interest-free loans from individuals according to their capacity to give was begun, complemented by a drive for increased regular weekly giving, to service these loans. Many loaned £50, and additionally promised to give £1 extra per week to allow these lump sums to be paid back with interest. In the event many who loaned relatively small sums eventually wrote them off.

After 50 per cent of the total had been raised by such means, augmented by regular fundraising events, the vicar began to look to charitable trusts for further funding. A retired member of the congregation combed through directories of trusts, eventually establishing a list of 35 whose giving policy appeared to match their project exactly. These were approached, describing the project, the nature of the congregation and the hard work and commitment which had already raised so much of the total. Many of these highly targeted applications were successful, raising further funds by a thousand or two at a time. A second, fall-back list of trusts was never needed.

A local councillor from within the community who was not a

church member but who sympathized with the project then identified a major source of funding from the European Union for which the church might be eligible to apply. A meeting was arranged and officials from the appropriate government office visited the site to discuss the possibilities. They felt that because the facilities would be open to the community as a whole, the project would be eligible for money from a special fund set up to help regenerate former coalfield areas. They were able to advise extensively through the application process, leading to the successful award of a grant which covered the remaining shortfall. The problem of subsequently raising matching funding, which faces so many projects which make EU or other statutory funds their first port of call, was never a problem for this church because of the intensive efforts and giving made by the congregation which had formed the first phase of their fundraising.

The whole campaign injected life into an ailing village community, using many different talents and involving many people. Coffee mornings were held every week, regularly raising £100. Those who opposed the project for any reason were visited personally to discuss their objections and to make sure they understood why the project was going ahead. Fundraising was spearheaded by the vicar, who spent some 30 per cent of his time on it initially, and who retained a deep involvement in order to maintain the momentum.

The project took two years from start to finish, leaving just the demolition of the old hall to complete it. The diocesan quota was paid in full throughout, and the diocese had been supportive of the project right from the beginning. In the end they stepped in to take care of this final task, probably recognizing what strenuous efforts had already been made to get so far. By this time the parish was in interregnum once again.

The new church rooms have been extensively used, allowing space for a Sunday School to build up, and are used midweek, e.g. for a local councillor's surgery and meetings of various community groups. The rooms are very lettable for parties and special functions. Through the winter the church actually meet in the larger room, saving a great deal of money on heating bills; smaller midweek services are also held in there. The project came in over target, allowing purchase of tables and chairs to fit the new rooms out. A new kitchen was donated as a 'gift in kind'.

Not many new people came into the church through the fundraising campaign, though a few became more committed and involved. Many in the community who were not churchgoers gave, and some Christians from outside the parish also made generous donations, often through the vicar's networks of contacts. The completion of the project transformed the facilities available to this small congregation, and gave them a good basis for mission and service to their community for decades to come.

Case study 4 **The community regeneration project**

Many would recognize the name of this urban area from the media coverage of the riots that flared into violence there in 1991. Much effort had already been channelled into the community to improve facilities and the quality of life for residents. These efforts were given new momentum in the wake of the riots. The church in the area had a long history of partnership with other agencies in projects seeking to address the problems faced by the residents and people of surrounding communities.

The Anglican parish which includes this estate consists of some 7,000 people, a number which is rising as new housing is built in one area of it. Housing is mixed in quality, with widespread refurbishment of some accommodation after the riots. There are a number of council estates in the parish, which are exhibiting various signs of social stress. The regular worshipping congregation numbers approximately 35 adults and a further 12 children.

Some years previously, an initiative under the former Community Development Programme had resulted in the setting-up of a project as a partnership between the local authority and the church. The church became the key partner in the funding package; however, as diocesan financial input subsequently diminished, the church input into the project correspondingly dwindled. The partnership now exists through one church being involved and essentially interpreting work in an urban setting to the wider Church – and vice versa. The vicar of the main Anglican parish in the area is still a trustee of the project, though not involved in active fundraising for it.

Some time after the riots, restructuring of the council led to the disappearance of official youth work in the area. In response to this loss, the vicar, together with various project workers, set up a new initiative to provide detached youth work for the three electoral wards in the immediate area, thus serving a wider area than the estate alone. Shortly after being set up, a 'Company Limited by Guarantee' was formed, with charitable status obtained five months later. The objectives were formally expressed as: 'to educate and assist young people up to the age of 25 who reside in the X, Y and Z wards of B county through their leisure time activities so to develop their physical, mental and spiritual capacities that they may grow into full maturity as individuals and members of society and that their conditions of life may be improved'. The Children's Project has its own set of aims and objectives, specifically relevant to the younger age of the children catered for.

Core funding came initially from a major grant from a charitable trust with which one of the directors of the projects had past links, through earlier work with HIV/Aids-related issues. Through this previous contact he was able to send an application directly to the trust, which was taken seriously because of his established credibility with them. After a visit from a trust representative, this trust made a commitment to give £50,000 per year for two years, to cover all core costs. The support of the 'Coalition against Crime' gave the project added status in the eyes of funders, as well as much valuable practical help in the early days, especially with book-keeping.

The emphasis initially focused on the lack of provision for 16–25-year-olds; however, soon afterwards the X Initiative Consortium (a local government precursor to City Challenge) identified a lack of children's play provision for under-13s. This lack caused a great deal of concern, especially in view of the earlier riots, in which children had participated. Two separate projects to deal with these respective needs were thus established, functioning as two halves of the one company. The Children's Project had its own set of aims and objectives. Once again, the advantage of working in an area with a high public profile for its needs meant that funding was relatively easy to obtain. At a meeting of the consortium, the vicar was asked how many youth workers would be needed to meet the need, and how much the project would cost. Doing rough calculations on the spot – the number of workers, the hours they would work, reasonable rate of pay per hour, plus adequate resources to support them with administrative backup and equipment – a sum was arrived at, and £30,000 for core costs was obtained from various statutory sources within 24 hours. This speed reflected both the credibility and the contacts achieved by the local vicar in previous work in the area. Further support for core costs for three to five years has come from other charitable trusts. It was the vicar's aim to set up a funding programme that would secure income for the projects for the first seven years of their lifetime.

In year two of the Detached Youth Work project, a major break-through in funding was made, when a match was made between the work of the project and the requirements of the European Social Fund (ESF). This opened exciting new doors for extra funding, though it also created immense problems, almost leading to the collapse of the project at one point. The key was to identify tangible training benefits for the young people passing through the project, training being the key priority for the ESF. Some work was needed in order to identify skills obtained by young people in their contact with the project, and their accreditation in a form that was acceptable to the ESF. Accreditation of various National Vocational Qualification (NVQ) levels for suitable activities was eventually linked to a national body.

The vicar was a key person in the obtaining of ESF money. He decided early on in the project to devote a day a week from regular parochial ministry to his involvement with the projects. He is one of three directors of the charitable company, and in addition is company secretary. However, filling the forms for the ESF application procedure was a major time commitment, absorbing a fortnight's work. He feels that had he not been by chance a geography graduate, he would have not had the expertise to fill them in correctly. A large amount of research was involved, both in statistics about the community and to accurately predict the number of young people who would be helped and the precise nature of the skills they would be able to impart. Little practical help was forthcoming from the local authority or the local EU secretariat, although a North-East organization set up to help voluntary organizations access EU money gave a great deal of support.

One of the major benefits of the ESF application procedure was that it forced all involved with the projects to assess carefully just what the project was achieving for the young people passing through their hands. Careful monitoring procedures have also been introduced by the youth workers employed by the project so that the effectiveness of their work can be tracked and if necessary demonstrated in tangible terms.

However, once a project has been accepted by the ESF, there can be significant problems in accessing the money. It is not unknown for payments to be delayed by months, often causing smaller projects desperate problems in terms of cashflow. Their workers need to be paid, but the money is just not there to do it. Late payments have cost the projects some £6,500 over the first three years of operations in interest repayments on loans taken out to cover this shortfall. At several points the projects have been in serious danger of collapse. At one point, the Employment Service found extra resources within its budget to train volunteers as part of the project. This experiment was extremely successful, with a high proportion of volunteers finding employment after a time of voluntary work with various agencies involved on the estate. It also brought £500 per volunteer into the project, tiding them over that particular funding crisis. Again it was the reputation of the projects and the contacts within local government that had been created which opened this particular avenue of funding. At another time, the project was within half an hour of being closed down, because bureaucracy was proving too great a barrier to the obtaining of a simple letter from the ESF to the projects' bank to assure them that the ESF funding had been formally approved, and would eventually be forthcoming. Without this written assurance the bank was unable to make loans to the project on the scale needed to fund their wages bill and other regular outgoings. Eventually after telephone conversations were exchanged at ministerial level in national government, the assurance was forthcoming. Once again personal contacts proved essential.

As the projects have developed, many other funders have supported them, sometimes for very specific aspects of their activities. Funding has come from a wide range of national and local trusts. The profile of the area has meant that it has been comparatively easy to attract funders to come to the area to see the needs and the value of the projects' work for themselves. Local companies have contributed little, partly because of the economic situation, and partly because such large sums are involved. An exception has been the project's bankers, who support the work by allowing an overdraft facility of £40,000. As the projects currently have an accumulated deficit of £18,000 this is extremely helpful.

The vicar still plays a key part in the fundraising for the projects, but feels that he does not have the time to spend on applications for sums of less than £10,000. The project workers themselves also spend some time cultivating relations with other agencies, and charities working in similar fields.

The projects are concerned, because of the cashflow problems induced by the ESF funding, to reduce their reliance on that source for the future. They are currently involved as part of a consortium in a bid for money from the National Lottery Charities Board. The lead partner in this is the local Resource Centre, although if successful a large proportion of the award would be directed towards the projects, because of their acknowledged success at using their money effectively. Other potential sources of statutory funding have also been identified. Here, just as in the case of the ESF funding, there is a need to break into a new funding system. The key will be to match the achievements of the projects in direct measurable terms for their clients with the precise framework within which that particular statutory source operates.

In many ways the projects impinge little on the life of the main parish church serving the community. Church membership is comparatively small, and though members are aware of the involvement their vicar has, they do not necessarily see the extent of his work behind the scenes. However, there is an awareness that the projects are doing good work, and that they address issues that the whole community agrees are important. The projects also provide an important context for ministry; there is always a two-way flow both of pastoral contacts with clients of the projects, and a referral to the projects of parishioners contacted through regular parochial ministry. This extends in some instances to the small-scale funding of the church's own work with children through the projects, for example Sunday School outings.

The vicar considers that any stronger structural link between the projects and local churches would not have been acceptable to the other agencies involved in the original planning of the scheme. However, his deliberate inclusion of the spiritual dimension of development for young people served by the projects means that the door is open for creative links between the church and the community through their lifetime. His own extensive involvement as a driving force for the health and stability of the community he serves certainly provides a pattern that may be of use in other deprived areas.

Case study 5 **The church extension**

This case study involves a small parish of some 5,000 souls, created as an independent parish six years ago. Formerly it was a daughter church of one of the city centre churches. The parish is made up of mainly private housing with a small amount of council accommodation. As part of a university city, it has a high student population, and many inhabitants derive their income directly or indirectly from the university or education. There is very little industry within the parish boundaries. The electoral roll numbers about 150. Many people have gifts and initiative but tend to have limited time and to ration their commitment accordingly. There is a rising proportion of over-fifties resident within the parish.

Plans for a church extension had been first mooted in the 1970s, with a groundswell of support from the congregation. A church hall was sited immediately opposite the church on the other side of the road. As this road (one of the main routes out of the city) became increasingly busy the need to have accommodation for children's groups, youth work and other meetings located on the same side as the church became more pressing. The church building lacked a toilet, and had only a small cramped vestry for meetings.

By the time a new vicar arrived on the scene, some years later, the existing hall was in need of attention, provoking re-examination of the situation. The decision was taken to sell the old church hall. This eventually raised £63,000. However the diocese made it clear that this money should be spent on a replacement church hall rather than any reordering or extension of the main church building. Thus when the church made plans for an extension, they were not allowed to use this money to start off their building fund. They were however allowed to use the interest to further the work of the parish.

The PCC began to work on plans for their extension with a respected local architect. The decision was made to go ahead with a full fundraising appeal, with £120,000 as the target needing to be raised to bring the scheme to reality. A sub-committee of the PCC was established to oversee the fundraising appeal. A simple brochure was produced and distributed to every house in the parish, with a response slip. The front cover featured the architect's drawing of the church with the extension in place; the inside left-hand page answered the questions why? what? when? and how much?, and the inside right page reproduced the architect's plans. The final page outlined ways in which people might give or loan money to support the project, together with examples of grossed up covenants, and gave the names of those on the appeal sub-committee. This sub-committee was chaired by the vicar, and included five other members drawn from the church, plus the church treasurer, who also took on the time consuming task of being treasurer for the appeal.

The appeal began one September, and by the end of the year some £89,000 had been pledged, mainly in the form of covenants. The following year this had risen to £122,000, and by the year after that to £150,000. The target eventually rose to £184,000, which was achieved in full after four years.

Many also gave by Gift Aid, which allowed the church immediate use of the money rather than having to wait four years to receive the full gross sum as with covenants. Members were presented with the target broken down into small portions within the reach of individuals; e.g. £150,000 actually represented just £1,000 from each person on the electoral roll. This could be realized in the form of covenants of just £5 per week (grossing over £1,300 per person over four years). This made the target seem less daunting.

Once half the funding was in place, a number of local trusts were approached for support, and three responded, contributing a further £4,100. One of the only businesses in the parish gave £100. The diocese contributed £15,000. The original mother church had a windfall itself through the sale of some land and gave £25,000.

Loans were also solicited, in order to enable the contractors to be engaged at an earlier stage. £23,000 came interest-free from individuals, £5,000 from a local church (interest-free to be repaid over five years) and £26,000 from the diocese, over five years at 5 per cent interest. In time, many of the individuals have decided that it has been right not to ask for their capital back, and loans have thus become gifts, which has been a considerable help.

The summer after the appeal started the vicar, who also chaired the appeal sub-committee, sent a letter to PCC members outlining the financial implications of the situation, prior to signing a contract with a firm of contractors to carry out the work, scheduled to begin within a month. This described the possible alternative scenarios if they proceeded with the work before the money was all raised. He pointed out that in the last resort members of the PCC carried the legal obligation to pay the builders personally. He asked for the PCC to take 'corporate legal and moral responsibility to ensure that the bills are paid'. The PCC courageously took the risk of this personal liability on board in their decision to proceed.

A fundraising group was convened to support the appeal by various events, such as barbecues, ceilidhs, sponsored walks, bring-and-buy sales. Some members of the congregation opened their homes for special meals, with guests paying a ticket price to attend. These all raised money from within the congregation itself, and promoted awareness, goodwill and a sense of teamwork. They raised comparatively little; some £8,000 over the years of the campaign. There was a strong line from the church leadership that forms of raffles or lotteries were not appropriate. Ultimately the group ceased to function, with a sense in some quarters that their activities had been restricted.

Towards the end of the campaign a mini-appeal was launched to raise the final £10,000. A simple card was distributed outlining the remaining need. This raised a further £5,000. The contractors completed the extension and were paid on time. The extension began to prove its worth very quickly for meetings, housegroups, and youth activities. The Sunday School in particular grew rapidly once the new facilities were in place. The final cost of the whole project was £183,314 and the final income was £183,365.

Postscript

The successful opening of their new church extension has not been the end of the story for this church. There remained the issue of a replacement church hall. The success of the fundraising appeal for the extension, and a desire to increase the effectiveness of the church's ministry into the local community have led to serious consideration of a second phase of fundraising, to build a new church hall/community centre to serve the parish. There is no other community centre building in the parish at present. The church is fortunate to have land on which to do this, and to have the proceeds of the sale of the original hall still intact to form the basis of a further appeal.

Discussions with representatives of the local community are now going ahead to establish the real needs that exist in the area, and ways in which a joint project with the church might meet these needs. Possibilities for work with pre-school children, community groups, evening classes and the elderly are all under discussion. At first the scheme was costed as in the region of £150,000. However, taking on the needs of the community in addition to those of the church has increased the scale of the plans, and the costs have risen accordingly into the region of £250,000. It is planned to seek funding from the local community more generally for this project, and to enlist the support of local councillors, etc. with a view to canvassing statutory sources of funding. Success in their first experience of fundraising has engendered the faith to go on to contemplate even greater endeavours.

Case study 6 **Real ale!**

This story begins with an ordinary pastoral contact, repeated many times over every year in most parishes in the Church of England. This particular parish is relatively rural, though on the edge of a commuter area. The electoral roll numbers about 260, and the parish comprises two villages, totalling around 9,500 population. A man had died, and the vicar took the funeral as part of his day-to-day ministry. The widow, now housebound, had been a churchgoer in earlier years, and he began to visit her home, taking her house communions regularly. Through this typical pastoral contact, the widow's son also came into contact with the Church. There was a desire to say 'thank you' to the Church for the pastoral support given. Subsequently the son raised the possibility of regular support for church funds from a rather unusual source.

His brother ran a micro-brewery in the West Country, winning awards for some of the range of beers developed and brewed there. One particular award winner, a high quality real ale, was not fulfilling its anticipated potential. The idea was to rename and relaunch this high quality ale, using marketing outlets in the parish and passing profits on to the church. The brewery would deliver it at cost price, using the church effectively as a wholesaler.

The vicar spent a few months thinking through this offer and consulting others, particularly senior diocesan staff. He felt that it would accord well with ancient traditions of mediaeval monasteries brewing their own beer and offering Christian hospitality to wayfarers. In fact, research proved that in mediaeval times his church had been a recognized stopping-off point for pilgrims en route to the local abbey! The suffragan bishop gave the scheme his blessing and undertook to back it publicly, using it as an opportunity to positively promote responsible use of alcohol, and the celebration of the good gifts of God in creation.

At the turn of the year the bishop contacted the vicar to let him know that he had an available date within a few weeks to come and launch the beer. This instilled a note of urgency to the proceedings, and the issue was debated formally and approved by the PCC. It was felt that it was a good idea in principle, as long as cashflow did not become a problem, and they were not drawn into buying more stock than they could pay for or easily sell. A member of the congregation with good public relations skills took on the task of raising the profile of the launch in the media and the general marketing of the project. Press releases were faxed out; quite a few newspapers ran with the story, from the local press to *The Times*, and the story was then picked up by television. The next week saw a whirlwind of media interest and activity for the vicar and his parishioners. He was provided with a chauffeur-driven car to go to London to take part in a live discussion on Radio Five Live, and two television companies sent reporters and cameras to the village to record short news items on the launch. The coverage was extensive, with little critical backlash. It was widely seen both within the parish and across the south of England.

A team of three people in the parish took on the promotion of actual sales of the beer, providing cases for special events and sales on a wholesale basis directly to the local inhabitants (a minimum three cases of 12 bottles each per transaction). The launch provoked a lot of interest and stimulated a substantial number of immediate sales; however, turnover then dipped over the summer, partly due to the busy lives of the volunteers concerned. One moved house, another was ill, inevitably affecting the time and energy they had to devote to promoting the beer. After the summer holidays a more strategic approach was adopted, and outlets in local shops and pubs were explored.

A change in the law is anticipated soon which will loosen the control major breweries have over their own pubs with regard to the sale of 'guest' beers, and this should lead to many more opportunities. On the other hand a difficulty with VAT legislation has meant that local off-licences have been less willing to sell, as the fact that they incur VAT on sale of the beer means that the profit they have to pass back to the church is minuscule.

The vicar found that the local magistrates' Licensing Department was extremely 'church-friendly', helping in many ways to introduce them to the complexities of the licensing laws. He was advised to take out one licence to cover the sale of alcohol on twelve different occasions within their area of jurisdiction. This enabled the church to plan social events at which the beer could be available well in advance. A degree of ecumenical liaison took place, whereby a beer tent selling the ale could be arranged at major events put on by other churches. The church was helped in its compliance with local authority regulations by another member of the congregation who was employed as a senior local government officer.

After the first few months of operations, it was clear that the whole project was a success from the parish's perspective. The brewery was happy to send the beer to the parish on a sale or return basis so the parish had to come up with very little actual cash to get the scheme under way. Stock was stored in private garages. The PCC delegated oversight of the finances of the scheme to a small group headed by the local government official. A separate bank account was set up into which income could be paid and out of which expenses relating to the sale of the beer could be met. At regular intervals there was a meeting with the church treasurer and funds were transferred into the church accounts. In the first month, due to the launch, £500 was made, though only another £500 came in over the next five months. The income has now settled down to a regular stream of about £200 per month.

In return for these benefits the church has encountered one or two problems. The initial setting-up of the project made heavy demands of the vicar's time and energy, although he has now stepped right back from this. The brewery remains happy with the arrangement, but there were a few problems with supply and demand in the early days, and the volunteers administering the sales have had to learn to think ahead and order well in advance to make sure that the brewery has adequate time to respond.

The intensive encounter with the media during the launch period represented a steep learning curve for the people of the parish and particularly the vicar. There were lessons he felt that had been learned the hard way which would influence his future relations with them. He was particularly concerned at just how easy it was to lose control of what was said and how difficult it was to influence the image that was eventually communicated to the public. He much preferred live interviews for this reason, as there was then no danger that his own carefully balanced viewpoint would end up on the cutting room floor, as happened to some extent with the TV interviews. Interestingly, the two television interviews felt to him like two very different experiences. In one, a good rapport was built up with the interviewer straight away, there was a useful discussion about the best way to approach the piece, he felt his concerns were addressed properly, and while not all the points he wished to make made it onto the screen, he felt the piece was fair. Subsequently this particular interviewer has begun attending church. In the other, he felt there was a prearranged agenda and approach, and that he had little room for manoeuvre. In hindsight he now wishes he had not agreed to a reconstruction of a 'typical service' to be recorded as part of this second piece, as this did not communicate a fair reflection of the worshipping life of his parish to the wider public. Sadder but wiser, he will assert his own perspective more forcefully on future occasions, and not feel that he should unquestioningly agree with all the suggestions of the media professionals.

In the parish the effect of the project and the media coverage continues to be felt. Most of it is positive; there has been a great raising of awareness both within the parish and beyond of the work of the Church. It has given widespread opportunities to present a Christian perspective on alcohol and other issues. Local people still stop him in the street to talk about it, months afterwards. A new sound system has been purchased for the church with the proceeds to date, allowing greater flexibility in services, and particularly giving the freedom to develop a less formal evening service attractive to young people. It has transformed the experience of church worship for many, especially the hard of hearing. Further funds will be diverted to help house and pay the expenses for the parish's next stipendiary curate.

The project has therefore fulfilled all the hopes raised when the concept was first suggested. It has raised the profile of the parish, encouraged debate about responsible patterns of drinking, and generated a stream of unallocated income into church funds. However, its very success means that in future months further issues may have to be addressed. Should the parish put time and energy into expanding the scheme? The church will need to balance the issue of additional income against the time and energy needed to promote the sales effectively. This in turn may lead to choices as to the contexts in which it may or may not be appropriate to sell the beer, and possibly to less direct control over who actually is consuming it and in what quantities. Maybe it will be appropriate to keep this as a comparatively small operation where the profit motive is not the be-all and end-all, and the tradition of those mediaeval monks centuries ago is allowed to shine on down the centuries, unsullied by the commercialism of the twentieth century.

Case study 7 **Planting a church**

This case study is based on the story of a redundant and derelict church building in west London, for which no one could find a satisfactory use. The building was unsafe, filled with dirt and rubble, and infested by pigeons.

For some considerable time, one of the largest evangelical charismatic Anglican churches in London had been looking for suitable sites for church-planting operations, believing this to be one of the most effective ways to promote church growth. These church plants involved the relocation of a section of the congregation, including one of the clergy, to reopen redundant buildings and establish a new growing church family to serve the local community. This church had already planted three other congregations successfully, and was keen to find more locations to repeat the process. Its leaders were in touch with the bishop and the diocesan secretary in the search for further opportunities.

Eventually one particular church, rundown for years and finally closed permanently, came to their attention. The decision to close was taken after many years during which church members had not had the resources to maintain the building properly, and after masonry actually began to fall from a column inside the church. The tiny remaining congregation was transferred to a neighbouring parish. The diocese, faced with the dilemma of how to deal with this situation of extended decline, had decided to divide the abandoned parish between two neighbouring churches. It had no immediate plans for the future of the building itself, which on closer inspection was completely decaying, damp and filthy.

Having heard of the existence of this empty building by chance at a meeting of local clergy and having visited the site, representatives of the parent church made contact with the bishop, suggesting that there might be a possibility for a fourth church plant there. They were encouraged to pursue the possibilities further. The curate from the church wishing to plant the new congregation (who would become its priest in charge if all went according to plan) then swung into action, excited by the potential of what he had seen. Enormous problems on a huge scale would obviously have to be tackled, so he set up a series of meetings consulting with local residents, with the council, with English Heritage, and anyone and everyone else who could possibly have a view to express or advice to impart. At the same time the parent church commissioned an architect to carry out a full survey; the report indicated a basically sound structure, but with major work needed on the roof, walls, floor, wiring and heating system. At least £600,000 would be needed before the building could be regarded as usable again. An initial paper about the project was submitted to the diocesan pastoral committee.

The diocese again responded positively, but required further negotiations with the vicar of the neighbouring parish, who had been providing pastoral cover, and the local area dean – and also required much more detail about any financial package to fund the restoration work. The intervening months before the next diocesan pastoral committee allowed time to carry out this additional research and write a supplementary paper. The upshot was a formal letter from the bishop inviting the curate of the parent church to become priest in charge of the abandoned parish, moving with his family into the vicarage there. Eventually 45 other adults from the parent church committed themselves to move with him to become the nucleus of a new congregation. In September services began in a rented school hall. By the following Easter there was a regular morning service, beginning to attract a few local families.

Meanwhile a full-scale fundraising operation was begun, linked to a phased programme of restoration work devised with the architect. Over £200,000 was raised quickly, in the form of major grants from the council and English Heritage (on the initiative of local residents who had thought it a tragedy that such a fine local building should be going to waste). These were matched by generous giving from the parent church and the diocese, and allowed contractors to be engaged to begin work on the roof and stonework.

The new priest in charge produced a fundraising brochure to use as a tool to bring in further funds. Not much came from local people, though there were a few examples of great generosity. Most individual gifts in the early days came from individual members of the parent church, who believed in the vision for the new church. Money was specifically given to help provide staff support – a part-time worker with a special emphasis on youth work and a music coordinator for one day a week – and some free financial and administrative advice was provided as a gift in kind.

From the beginning, the restored church building was seen as a focus which would draw together people from all parts of what is a very diverse community. The local area had few meeting places already in existence, and some sectors of the population remained isolated. The building was to be a place where all kinds of people would be welcomed: youngsters, refugees, the homeless and deprived, alongside the population from more prosperous areas within the parish.

Working parties began clearing out the rubbish and rubble. Over Easter the congregation was able to move into the church, though for many months they moved from area to area within the building as restoration work took place around them. With no heating it was sometimes bitterly cold; their only lighting came from one arc lamp, but the small congregation remained in good heart.

Fundraising continued with an evening reception in the church itself, attended by the bishop – a high-profile event with an overt fundraising content. After a lot of internal debate, an application to the National Heritage Memorial Fund of the National Lottery had been submitted the previous May, and just before Christmas it was announced that this had been successful, and that £430,000 had been awarded – effectively 75 per cent of the outstanding balance still needed. This allowed work to proceed much faster than would otherwise have been the case.

Construction work could now continue, creating a hall on ground level within the building which would be open to the community for mothers and toddler groups, art workshops, music events. Rooms created upstairs would house a nursery school, and be used by refugee groups from the local area, specifically Zaireans, Ethiopians and Somalis. A midweek evening youth club was started, attracting 80 youngsters, and the church's youth leader worked alongside the local council and the Police running holiday clubs over the summer for teenagers.

A couple of years later the bishop returned as visiting preacher in a

191

fully renovated, warm and well-lit church to induct the priest in charge as vicar of the parish. Over £900,000 had been raised and the programme of work was almost completed. The regular congregation had grown to 120 and was attracting new visitors from the area, curious to see just what was going on inside this local landmark. Other local residents passed through the doors each week to attend meetings and community activities. As the bishop concluded in his address that night, 'This is a night to celebrate, but it's only the beginning.'

Case study 8 Villages youth project

Phase one

This story had its beginning when a particular need for youth facilities was identified in a village a few miles from the coast in a rural area of England. An influx of tourists in the holiday season meant that a couple of small neighbouring holiday resorts, which had seen better days, were a focus of some activities in the summer months, but in the winter there was little for most youngsters to do other than to hang around a bus shelter in the village street, which did not even have a seat in it because of vandalism problems. A village youth club already existed, but only met for one evening a week. High bus fares (with virtually no night-time service) and poor employment prospects led to boredom and general disaffection with life. In recent years problems with drugs, alcohol and solvent abuse had begun to surface. Other local villages shared exactly the same problem.

The catalyst which led to change was a man who had recently moved into the village, who expressed a real concern for these youngsters and who began to spend time on the streets with them, listening to them and building up their trust. His motivation was an outworking of his very real Christian faith. They told him they wanted somewhere with minimum supervision where they could meet, talk, and 'do their own thing'. These young people were not being touched by the existing work of the church, which concentrated on church-affiliated youth organizations largely serving the children and teenagers of existing church families.

By the end of the year, the imagination of the young people themselves had been engaged. They formed their own committee and started fundraising to buy a double-decker bus, hoping to convert it into a mobile coffee bar to serve the different villages in the area. A sponsored lorry pull was followed in turn by a pool marathon, and cooperation with representatives of the Prince's Trust led to further initiatives. An open meeting in the village identified some local adults who were also drawn into support for the work, and an adult committee followed. The diocesan youth officer was consulted for advice. With the help of an interest-free loan and a grant from a major charitable trust and some local businesses, a bus was purchased. The man with the original vision for the project was appointed as an unpaid project worker. He began to work with other volunteers who had the practical skills necessary to reorder the bus. Upstairs seats were removed to house a TV, video, hi-fi, games and an office. Downstairs became a coffee bar with seats and tables. By the end of the year the bus was ready to take to the road, complete with stunning external graffiti artwork, and a generator donated by a local company.

Early the next year the bus was formally launched. Although the project was not a church project as such, it was manned by Christians on a voluntary basis for four nights a week, covering three villages; subsequently a fourth village asked to be involved and was included. The project sought and obtained affiliation to the diocesan Children and Youth Committee. Attendances were good. In addition to their regular nights, some young people attended a residential time away at a youth centre in the county, and other initiatives away followed, including a trip to the FA Cup Final. A music workshop was set up which led to the formation of a band, who later played at the village carnival, having been equipped by a grant from the Prince's Trust. The need for a car to transport equipment and assist the project worker was met by the provision of a loan car from the village garage.

A break-in and theft of equipment was a major setback, but renewed fundraising through events such as a car boot sale and a Sixties night helped replace the items lost. The project worker developed his role working on the streets with young people, helping with drug- and alcohol-related problems.

The bus soon became a regular sight around the villages. The project worker was now carrying out his role under an Employment Action contract as a placement to develop skills in working with young people. A video project was undertaken with help from an Arts Council grant, which involved young people and professionals working together. CB enthusiasts took an interest in the bus and helped the young people fundraise with a fun day and a car-pull.

However, the very success of the project was causing stresses and strains. The needs of the young people became more demanding as the quality of their involvement deepened. Issues of substance abuse, homelessness and crime surfaced, leading to the need for closer links with agencies such as the Probation Service, Social Services, the Police and the Youth Enquiry service. An open day for various agencies was held to promote better communications. Partly as a result of these increased demands and partly because of the conclusion of the volunteer youth worker's placement, a review was held to identify a new series of aims and objectives for the project. It was decided that the time had come to appoint a full-time professional youth worker.

Phase two

The committee consulted widely, looking at other similar schemes including both county council and Christian youth work projects. Their aim was to produce a realistic job description and develop a strategic plan to attract funding for the youth worker's salary. The long process of applying for registered charity status was begun at this point; hitherto the project had worked under the diocesan Charity Commission number. Some new blood was drafted on the committee and one of the local clergy also took a more direct interest in supporting the project.

A crucial point in the proceedings was reached when the diocesan youth officer suggested an approach to a particular national charitable trust with an interest in youth work. After contact with one of the trust's representatives, the outcome was a five-year package of funding to pay a youth worker to work part-time on the project, with the understanding that the worker would be released to pursue professional qualifications alongside his or her work by distance learning. The trust laid down firm criteria for the running of the project, with clear systems of administration and responsibility, but this was perceived as a positive advantage to the local committee rather than in any sense inhibiting their work. They felt much more secure in their role because of the wide experience that was now open to them through the trust.

A weekend course away for members of the committee helping them to learn how to be effective managers was extremely valuable, especially as the employment of a salaried worker instead of a volunteer subtly altered the whole dynamic of the project. The treasurer now had a greatly increased workload, having to manage such matters as National Insurance, tax and pension provision, as well as the usual basic income and expenditure and incidental expenses. Some volunteer helpers were less inclined to maintain their commitment at the same level once a professional was appointed, feeling they were no longer needed. There was also a sense for a while that they no longer needed to try to generate income from fundraising because the costs were covered so extensively and for so long by the major grant, supplemented by a few smaller donations from trusts and companies.

A rigorous and thorough application procedure attracted some very high calibre candidates, and an appointment was subsequently made, although a change in domestic circumstances for this individual led to his departure. This meant that within twelve months the whole procedure had to be repeated. A second worker is now in place, bringing a host of skills and talents to her role, not least of which has been the newly acquired ability to drive a double-decker! The project is working well and fulfilling the original vision.

However, as the end of the five-year funding programme appears on the horizon, the issue of the way forward for the longer-term future will have to be addressed again, and the members of the management committee are beginning to turn their attention to securing a broader financial base of support. Aspects of the project may be relatively easy to fund – for example where drugs and AIDS advice are involved – but there will still be a basic need for ongoing core funding. The committee feels the need for good fundraising advice keenly, having learned the hard way that fundraising through events and activities is hard work and can be a high-risk route to uncommitted income. One of the best avenues of hope may lie in the excellent relationships built up by the current project worker with statutory and semi-statutory agencies in the area. Committee members remain enthusiastic, and are determined to do everything possible to ensure the continued survival of a project that has made such a qualitative difference to the lives of youngsters in the area.

Case study 9 **Rebuilding after fire**

Five years before this case study came to be written, a church situated in a leafy suburb of London burned down overnight. The glow could be seen for miles across the city skyline. In the morning only the tower and some sections of wall remained standing, the rest of the building reduced to charred and smoking rubble. Stunned parishioners gathered round the ruins, finding it hard to take in the extent of the sheer devastation.

Understandably the impact on the congregation was enormous, with a sense of shock and bereavement that could only be worked through together in time. It touched not only church members but many in the community who had loved and valued the familiar landmark in their midst. The bishop was supportive by his presence in the aftermath of the fire and there was a general sense of a tragedy shared.

However, the regular ministry of the church had to go on, and the immediate question of where to meet for worship was resolved by use of a parish hall about a quarter of a mile away from the original site, with a chapel elsewhere in the parish linked to a schools foundation being used for the occasional offices, weddings and funerals, etc. Traditional prayerbook worship was catered for in the chapel, while the more adventurous forms of worship to which the main congregation had become accustomed were possible in the parish hall.

The 'Phoenix Fund' was launched immediately in order to enable the church to continue to function with even the barest of necessities in their new environment. They had lost everything – books, robes, music, and had many pressing immediate needs. This first fundraising push was to become the springboard for a subsequent more substantial fundraising operation. At this early stage gifts came in from some surprising sources, from those who had heard about the tragedy and were touched by it.

The next step was to initiate the insurance claim procedure. The church had been well insured, but not to the extent that 100 per cent of the costs were covered. From the earliest stages it was unanimously accepted that the church would not be rebuilt on the same plans as the original building, and this led to detailed and at times difficult negotiations as to what might or might not be covered by the policy. The church people wanted a totally new design, with seating for about the same number as the original building, but designed to afford far more flexibility. The need for new money to complement the sum received from the insurance company was apparent from the earliest stages.

Once the insurance money had been received this was banked to allow an income stream from the interest until it was needed to pay actual bills – a valuable source for cashflow. Meanwhile, thought was given to the actual shape and style of the new building. Services in the hall gave experience of worship in a semi-circle and the feeling grew that the replacement building should allow worship in the round. An architect was advertised for, and a church committee, using expertise from some church members with relevant professional experience, eventually selected seven from a list of over forty interested applicants. These seven were asked to submit a description of how they would go about rebuilding the church, and the list was narrowed down to three and then to just one. The chosen architect had taken the opportunity to worship several times with the congregation to ensure that he was fully in tune with their ethos and aspirations. A thorough brief was then prepared for him, seeking flexibility, excellent sight lines and good ancillary accommodation. The architect felt strongly that light should be used in the new building to draw out a sense of the numinous in worship.

Alongside this progress, the inevitable need to carry other interested parties along with them necessitated extensive consultations, discussions and meetings: with the diocesan advisory committee, English Heritage, local councillors, the planning department, and the public. A faculty was needed just to pull the remainder of the ruins down, and it was not until a year after the fire that the site could actually be cleared. Investigations then revealed that arson had been the cause of the fire. Some small mementoes of the earlier building were retrieved at this point.

As the architect and church moved ahead towards a stunning new design for the rebuilding, departing from tradition with extensive use of glass and light, the radical nature of the proposed design attracted criticism in some quarters and enthusiastic support in others. Echoes of the old building were incorporated where possible to provide reminders of the past and a sense of continuity. Some of the original stonework was used in a garden of remembrance outside the church, the ancient font which escaped the fire having been discarded outside the building was

197

brought back into use, and a cross was movingly fashioned from some charred timbers.

Objectors inside and outside the church were vocal at times, and constructive criticism was listened to carefully, sometimes leading to modifications. Some objectors were won over, others continued to oppose. It took two and a half years to receive diocesan approval for the plans, and the local authority's planning department finally passed the scheme only on the chairman's casting vote. At last the church was in a position to go out and fundraise for the remaining sum they needed, with a firm proposal to lay before prospective funders.

The fundraising was directed towards those aspects of the scheme which the insurance would not cover: provision of a reception area, lounge, kitchen, choir vestry and offices, and a doubling of space available for a suite of community rooms which had been situated next door to the church and which had not been damaged by the fire. To these were added the cost of suitable lighting, a sound system and other equipment. The Phoenix Fund had raised £70,000, some of which had been spent straight away. This new phase of the campaign was put at £300,000, although costs continued to rise and the full sum needed would eventually be in the region of £400,000. The decision was made not to engage a professional fundraiser. However, a project director, a newly retired former churchwarden, was employed to oversee all aspects of the scheme. It took an enormous amount of his time, but proved to be a vital role.

The church owned a building elsewhere in the parish which it leased to the local health authority, generating an income stream which had been used from time to time to finance capital projects. A capital sum from this source gave a boost to the funds. A small steering group was established to raise extra money, largely through events. Many individuals from the church gave, some using Gift Aid, though not many chose to covenant gifts on a longer-term basis. This may have been because the church congregation is very mobile with a lot of members moving to the area for a number of years then moving on. However, a more positive effect of this mobility was the amount of support which came from former members who were traced and contacted about the need to rebuild.

The Arts Council was involved in financing a specific part of the rebuilding programme. This involved the stained glass for the main east and west windows, which were commissioned by the church from an

artist who lived in the parish. The whole process from design to instal-
lation of the windows was made into an education and training project,
and the windows were displayed before they were put in place. This
training dimension led the Arts Council to give a grant of £46,000 out
of the total £50,000 cost. Although the source of the funding was ultimately from the National Lottery, this was not a particular issue for this
church. Extensive applications were made to trusts and companies, but
the results were not hugely successful; some £11–12,000 in grants and
a little sponsorship for fundraising events were received. The church is
not in an urban priority area, though like many areas of London comparatively comfortable housing exists alongside much poorer areas, and
the parish is definitely mixed in nature. A little merchandising also took
place, with greetings cards and mugs bringing in a steady small income.

The campaign is now in the difficult final stages. The building took
18 months to construct but is now open for use. There is a degree of
donor fatigue among the regular congregation, allied to the extreme
mobility of the membership. The 20 per cent turnover every year means
that a substantial number of regular worshippers do not now remember
the former building. Alongside the fundraising for the building, the
parish has had to face an ever-rising diocesan quota, which has gone up
some 35 per cent since the fire to £106,000 per annum. The final bills
will be paid by taking out loans. The diocese has agreed to loan up to
£200,000 at bank rate if necessary, and a 'Happy Birthday Appeal' on
the first anniversary of the church taking possession of the new facilities was made to service this borrowing. Appeals have also been made
to the congregation for interest-free loans as opposed to further gifts.

The final fundraising push will concentrate outside the immediate
congregation, seeking support from those in the local community who
stand to benefit from the enhanced facilities of the new building. A
series of events for them are planned – bazaars, barn dances, mara-
thons, auctions of promises and other such activities. Community use
of the building is growing; the main church is a beautiful venue for the
performance of music, and use of the suite of community rooms is rising. The parish hall has reverted to its former uses once more, and is
fully let out; lying alongside a local school it is a popular venue for
clubs, societies and uniformed organizations.

The whole process from disaster to new building has had a profound
effect on the congregation. In the early days they were bound together
by the common experience of shock, and held together well. A few

determined objectors to the rebuilding plans eventually left, but there was a lot of enthusiasm for the chosen scheme, and pleasurable surprise at the beauty and lightness of the building, and the release of such a lot of space for worship and ancillary purposes. The loss of the church's ASB service books in the fire, and the experience of months of worship in the parish hall, have reinforced an existing trend to look creatively at liturgical possibilities, leading to the design of their own orders of service. The congregation regularly uses a wide range of material produced by the Liturgical Commission, often linked to the seasons of the year. The flexibility of the building has lent itself to support this trend.

Since the building was reopened a lot of new people have been attracted to join the church, some probably attracted through the newsletter publicizing progress which went into every house in the parish at intervals through the process. A book telling the story of the church since the fire is under production and will be printed by a local firm. What began as unmitigated and totally unexpected tragedy has led to the provision of superb new facilities and a distinctive and beautiful place of worship. It has been a long hard road for all those involved, but out of disaster has come new birth and great blessing.

Case study 10 **African development trust**

The X Development Trust is a registered charity formed by Christians to 'assist in relief, rehabilitation, and development in X [a country in Africa] in cooperation with the Church and other organizations'. Its roots lay in the Lambeth Conference of 1988, when the bishop from the region spoke there of the devastation and civil disorder within his diocese. The new government of the time were imposing a harsh regime to counter pockets of rebel activity, and at the same time a neighbouring tribe and other bandits were carrying out raids, further impoverishing the people. Later the army forced a large proportion of the population into large camps, hoping to crush all resistance. By the time they were allowed home their farms were neglected and it was too late to plant. Famine was widespread and the whole fabric of society was shattered. Early efforts to help the situation in the form of the X Relief Campaign were followed by the formation of the Trust, which also incorporated two existing organizations supporting a local leprosy centre and a hospital.

The X Development Trust is open to anyone who wishes to support its work and who pays the minimal annual subscription. The day-to-day running is in the hands of a general secretary in the UK, supported by an executive committee meeting every 2–3 months. Members are drawn from those who have worked as expatriates in the country concerned and members of the X community living in England. Since its beginning the trust has concentrated on relief work, support for the leprosy centre and the hospital, involvement in the president of the country's 'Presidential Commission for X', evangelism, support for AIDS programmes, reconciliation (between warring factions), schools and local churches.

In the early days the trust was successful in raising comparatively large sums from the British government (Overseas Development Agency), Comic Relief and Christian Aid, as well as from those who were motivated for personal reasons to support the area. However, in time, as the immediate crisis passed and a measure of peace returned to the area, income dropped and the amount of help the trust could give was radically curtailed, despite the severe long-term needs that remained.

One Midlands UK diocese embarked on a special 'Partners in Restoration' project, in order to strengthen the sense of partnership established earlier when a team of nine had visited that area of Africa to help the people in extending a girls' secondary school. The aim of this new project, at the invitation of the local bishop in Africa, was to complete the building and equipping of two science labs, the library and an extra classroom, as well as to run a conference for all of the clergy and some lay leaders. In doing so it was hoped to involve far more people than in the first visit as well as to raise considerable funds. Applications were received from individuals to take part in two teams. Twenty people were eventually selected and after training were able to visit and to contribute practical help of various kinds.

A rolling programme of fundraising events and activities in parishes across the diocese in the UK began, usually conceived and put together by concerned individuals in individual churches. A publicity officer was appointed to generate maximum media awareness of all this activity, and the project organizer produced a regular newsletter for supporters. This was a simple A5 leaflet, packed with news, giving details about progress with the project and with fundraising, advertising supporting materials available to people wishing to help, and supplying prayer points. The newsletter editor became a key point of contact and communication between all the different fundraising initiatives. This helped keep the cause in the public eye, and maintained the personal links which were always a key to the success of this campaign.

As well as personal donations, many people came up with extremely inventive ideas to raise funds. One man decided to eat more simply during his lunchbreaks at work, giving the unspent money to the fund. Another couple with catering experience held a series of dinner parties in their home. Raffles, cake sales, sales of work, merchandising of greetings cards, concerts, dances, special services, and sponsored activities were held. One supporter got himself arrested by prior arrangement with the Police (allegedly for activities contrary to the 'Deep Pockets and Short Arms Act 1930'!). He was sponsored to spend the night in custody at the police station, and raised further funds from solicitors and others passing through the station.

The manager of the national airways of the country concerned allowed each team member to take an extra 15kgs of hand luggage with them, allowing building tools, extra books and equipment to be taken directly into the country. Before, containers of books and medical equipment had been sent in advance by sea, but the high cost of import taxes meant that it was better this time to purchase further books, science equipment and medicines etc. in Africa. Extra luggage allowances were extremely helpful.

The project eventually raised over £50,000, which was all channelled through the trust. The organizer felt that this was primarily due to direct personal contacts and knowing exactly how and where the money was to be used, as well as good communications. It is very doubtful whether such a large sum of money would have been raised if it had not been linked to people actually going to the area to work on a specific project, so enabling hundreds of people to feel personally involved and committed. However, she also writes, 'But of course God was very much at work, releasing people to give sacrificially, not just in terms of money. We shall never know the hours of committed prayer that went into the project.'

Useful sources of information

Publications

Charities Aid Foundation
(publishers of *The Directory of Grant Making Trusts, Charity Magazine*, etc.)

Charities Aid Foundation
Kings Hill, West Malling, Kent ME19 4TA

Charity Magazine
48 George Street, London W1H 5RF

Directory of Social Change
(publishers of *A Guide to Major Trusts, Trust Monitor, Corporate Citizen*, etc.)

Publications Dept, Directory of Social Change
24 Stephenson Way, London NW1 2DP

Professional Fundraising
TM&D Press Ltd
39–41 North Road, London N7 9DP

Third Sector
Third Sector Subscriptions Department, Arts Publishing International Ltd
FREEPOST LON 6577, London E1 7BR

UK Christian Handbook
Paternoster Publishing
PO Box 777, Carlisle CA3 0QR

General

Charity Commission
St Alban's House, 57–60 Haymarket, London SW1Y 2QX
also at:
2nd Floor, 20 Kings Parade, Queens Dock, Liverpool L3 4DQ
and at:
Woodfield House, Tangier, Taunton, Somerset TA1 4AY

English Heritage
23 Savile Row, London W1X 1AB

Inland Revenue
Somerset House, Strand, London WC2R 1LB

Inland Revenue (Charity Division)
St John's House, Merton Road, Bootle, Merseyside L69 4EJ

Institute of Charity Fundraising Managers
Market Towers, 1 Nine Elms Lane, London SW8 5NQ

National Association for Councils of Voluntary Service
3rd Floor, Arundel Court, 177 Arundel Street, Sheffield S1 2NU

National Council for Voluntary Organizations
Regent's Wharf, 8 All Saints Street, London N1 9RL

National Lottery Charities Boards
England:
St Vincent House, 16 Suffolk Street, London SW1Y 4NL
Northern Ireland:
Hildon House, 30–34 Hill Street, Belfast BT1 2LB
Scotland:
Norloch House, 36 Kings Stables Road, Edinburgh EH1 2EJ
Wales:
Ladywell House, Newtown, Powys SY16 1JB

NB Contact details for local authorities, councils, Police, Training and Enterprise Councils, etc. should be easily available in your local telephone directory.

Websites

CaritasData Ltd
(free information on top 5,000 charities) http://www.caritasdata.co.uk

Charities Aid Foundation
http://www.charitynet.org

Charity Commission
http://www.charity-commission.gov.uk

Charity Magazine
http://www.charitynet.org/news

Directory of Social Change
http://www.d-s-c.demon.co.uk

European Commission
http://www.cec.org.uk

Funderfinder
http://www.funderfinder.org.uk

Inland Revenue
http://www.open.gov.uk/inrev/irhome.htm

National Council for Voluntary Organisations
http://www.vois.org.uk/ncvo/

National Lottery Website
(with links to all boards) http://www.lottery.culture.gov.uk/

UK Fundraising*
http://www.fundraising.co.uk

UK Government
http://www.open.gov.uk

* Created by Howard Lake, who has also written *Direct Connection's Guide to Fundraising on the Internet* (Aurelian Information Ltd), a useful source of information for those seeking to make the most of the resources the Internet offers to fundraisers; it has many useful links to other relevant sites.